Young Adult Authors

Christine Wilcox

ReferencePoint Press®

San Diego, CA

© 2017 ReferencePoint Press, Inc.
Printed in the United States

For more information, contact:
ReferencePoint Press, Inc.
PO Box 27779
San Diego, CA 92198
www.ReferencePointPress.com

LIBRARY OF CONGRESS CATALOGING-IN-PUBLICATION DATA

Names: Wilcox, Christine.
Title: Young adult authors / by Christine Wilcox.
Description: San Diego, CA : ReferencePoint Press, Inc., 2017. | Series: Collective biographies series | Audience: Grades 9 to 12. | Includes bibliographical references and index.
Identifiers: LCCN 2016013751 (print) | LCCN 2016014565 (ebook) | ISBN 9781682820360 (hardback) | ISBN 9781682820377 (eBook)
Subjects: LCSH: Young adult literature, American--Juvenile literature. | Young adult literature, English--Juvenile literature. | Authors, American--Biography--Juvenile literature. | Authors, English--Biography--Juvenile literature.
Classification: LCC PS490 .W54 2017 (print) | LCC PS490 (ebook) | DDC 810.9/9283--dc23
LC record available at http://lccn.loc.gov/2016013751

CONTENTS

The New Golden Age of Young Adult Literature

S ince the turn of the millennium, young adult literature has achieved unprecedented popularity. Young adult titles now regularly top the best-seller lists and attract readers of all ages. Some experts have said that the young adult genre has single-handedly kept the flagging publishing industry afloat in the United States over the last decade. The industry reported that sales rose a whopping 22.4 percent between 2013 and 2014, while sales of adult books were down 3.3 percent. Though adult book sales made a comeback in 2015, young adult novels are still extremely popular, and most experts say they will remain so for the foreseeable future.

The History of Young Adult Fiction

There have always been books that appeal to readers in their teens. Novels like J.D. Salinger's *The Catcher in the Rye* (1951) and William Golding's *The Lord of the Flies* (1954) have been standards in high school curriculums for decades. But in the 1960s and 1970s, the term "young adult literature" started gaining popularity in the publishing industry as a way to distinguish children's literature from the edgier, issue-driven fiction written for teen readers. Gritty novels like S.E. Hinton's *The Outsiders* (1967) and Robert Cormier's *The Chocolate War* (1974) are standouts of this period, as are the young adult works of Judy Blume, such as *Are You There, God? It's Me, Margaret* (1970).

In the next two decades, young adult narratives tended to be driven by a single issue, tackling controversial topics like rape, teen pregnancy, violence, drug use, and suicide. Most were slim volumes that were not marketed to—or read by—adults, and very few made much money for authors or publishers. Then, in 1997, J.K. Rowling published the first book in her wildly successful *Harry Potter* series, which appealed to middle-school readers (ages eight to twelve), young adults (ages twelve to eighteen), and adult readers alike. Suddenly, publishers realized they could market young adult fiction to all ages. The new golden age of young adult literature had begun.

What Makes a Book "Young Adult"?

Today, there are very few rules as to what makes a book "young adult." However, one thing common to almost all young adult fiction is that the protagonist or narrator is a teenager and the story is told from his or her point of view. The teenager often faces various challenges that usually help shape his or her identity. According to young adult author Patrick Ness, young adult fiction tends to be about "finding your boundaries . . . and maybe stepping over those boundaries. It's about discovery."[1]

Common features of recent young adult fiction are strong female protagonists, absent or dysfunctional parents, and love triangles. For instance, the hugely popular *Twilight* saga by Stephanie Meyer features a love triangle comprising a werewolf, a vampire, and the protagonist—a teenage girl with an absent mother and a difficult relationship with her father. Many young adult novels involve the theme of a hero's journey, and most—but not all—end on a hopeful note.

*There are few rules when it comes to **young** adult literature, but common characteristics do exist. **Stories** are often told from the point of view of a teen narrator or protagonist who faces challenges that will help shape **his** or **her** identity.*

Diversity in Young Adult Fiction

While young adult fiction is now the mainstay of many publishing houses, there has been little progress in the number of young adult titles about multicultural teens. In 2013 in the United States, only 10 percent of children's and young adult books had multicultural content, even though 37 percent of the population consists of people of color. In response to this, authors Ellen Oh and Malinda Lo organized the We Need Diverse Books campaign in 2014, which works to encourage the publishing industry to promote books that reflect diversity. Other organizations took up the call as well, and librarians and educators have responded by promoting titles that feature nonwhite characters, such as Sherman Alexie's *The Absolutely True Diary of a Part-Time Indian* (2007). Young adult literature that reflects sexual and gender diversity has made less headway, however; while there was a 59 percent increase in lesbian, gay, bisexual, and transgender (LGBT) titles in 2014, there were still only forty-seven titles published by mainstream publishers in the United States.

Experts say that diversity in young adult literature is important because it helps multicultural readers connect with books in a meaningful way. But these books are not just for minorities. "In our growing multicultural world, kids need to know what it is to empathize with people that are different," says editor Stacy Whitman. She also notes that fantasy and science fiction—both very popular genres within young adult literature—are excellent ways to portray diversity. "You're already putting yourself in a setting that is already so different,"[2] she explains.

Pushing Boundaries

Young adult fiction is such a financial force in publishing that it will dominate the industry for some time to come. While trends in young adult books may swing from vampires to dystopian fiction to realism, the best young adult fiction will continue to push boundaries. And publishers seem open to that. "Conversations are happening in YA [young adult literature] that you're not seeing anywhere else,"[3] says bookseller Kimberly Jones, who notes that books for teens often take more risks than adult fiction. Like all great literature, the best young adult fiction has something to say about today's complex world. And more people are listening than ever before.

> "Conversations are happening in YA that you're not seeing anywhere else."[3]
>
> —Bookseller Kimberly Jones.

CHAPTER 1

Walter Dean Myers

As a boy, Walter Dean Myers had a hard time figuring out who he was. He was big for his age, loved sports, and was always ready for a fight. But he was also a voracious reader and talented writer—traits that set him apart from the other boys. However, as much as he loved reading, the characters in the books he read were nothing like him: an African American boy growing up in Harlem. Myers did not know where he fit in, and this struggle with his identity plagued him in his teens and early twenties.

Once Myers realized he could write about his own childhood experiences as an African American, he found his identity. He wrote more than one hundred books for children and young adults before his death in 2014. His books deal with the challenges faced by African American children growing up in big cities—topics that were mostly absent from books for young people. Because of this, Myers is credited with changing the nature of young adult literature, making it more diverse, inclusive, and realistic. According to Susan Katz, president of HarperCollins Children's Books, "Walter's many award-winning books do not shy away from the sometimes gritty truth of growing up. He wrote books for the reader he once was, books he wanted to read when he was a teen. He wrote with heart and he spoke to teens in a language they understood."[4]

Growing Up in Harlem

Walter Milton Myers was born on August 12, 1937, in Martinsburg, West Virginia, just 10 miles (16 km) from the plantation where his ancestors once labored as slaves. His mother died shortly after she gave birth to his younger sister, Imogene, when Walter was only eighteen months old. His father, George Myers, was left with seven children to raise, which included two daughters from a previous marriage to Florence Dean. After his wife's death, George contacted Florence and she and her new husband, Herbert, agreed to raise Florence's two daughters and to informally adopt Walter.

Because the Deans were a mixed-race couple—Florence was of German and Native American descent and Herbert was African American—they settled in Harlem, a neighborhood in New York City that was predominantly black and more accepting to married couples like the Deans. At the time, Harlem was a vibrant community, home to African Americans of all walks of life, from working-class people like the Deans to doctors, judges, and other professionals. While the Deans did not consider themselves to be poor, by today's standards they were; Herbert earned only janitor's wages, and Florence often had to clean houses or take on factory work to make ends meet. Despite these challenges, Myers had fond memories of his childhood and of the Deans, and he later adopted the pen name "Walter Dean Myers" to honor his adoptive parents.

> **"He spoke to teens in a language they understood."[4]**
>
> —Susan Katz, president of HarperCollins Children's Books.

A Struggle with Identity

Walter discovered when he was very young that he loved reading and writing. He began to write poetry in elementary school, and his teachers, recognizing his talent, encouraged him to keep writing. However, at the time, only white authors were taught in schools. Since he was never exposed to authors of color, Walter began to believe that to be an important poet—like Lord Byron or Elizabeth Barrett Browning—one had to write about issues that concerned the white upper class. "In truth, everything in my life . . . that was personal and had value was white,"[5] he recalled. Because of this, he decided that the contemporary black authors who lived in Harlem—such as Langston Hughes and Zora Neale Hurston—were second rate. Of Langston Hughes, he said, "He didn't fit my stereotype of what serious writers should be. . . . He wasn't writing about Venice."[6]

In the seventh grade, Walter was placed in a class for gifted students. This helped him get accepted to Stuyvesant, a prestigious public high school. During his high school years, his family became dysfunctional—his father had fallen into a depression, and his mother was drinking and gambling. Walter sometimes did not have money for clothing or lunch, and he missed a lot of school. When he did attend class, he was not a model student— he rarely did his homework and frequently got in trouble. By the time he was sixteen and a senior, he was out of school for weeks at a time.

Walter's struggles with his identity—with who he was and what he wanted to be—were becoming more pronounced. In the mid-1950s, many African Americans were uneducated, and the only jobs open to them were low-paying manual work. Walter rejected this identity and instead aspired to be a great thinker and writer. However, the more he learned about the world, the more he came to believe that no one would take an African American seriously as an intellectual. When he realized that his family could not afford to send him to college, he fell into despair. His only comforts were his writing and his books. "I read voraciously," he said of this time, "spending days in Central Park reading when I should have been going to school."[7]

> "Everything in my life . . . that was personal and had value was white."[5]
>
> —Walter Dean Myers

Escape to the Army

Walter's growing belief that the only work open to him was manual labor made him angry and rebellious. At sixteen, he began working as a drug courier and had several violent encounters with local gang members. Then, inspired by the war poetry of Rupert Brooke and films about World War II, he decided to become a soldier. Walter felt like a failure and he wanted a fresh start—even if that meant that he would die in battle. "I wanted to get away from home, away from Harlem, away from anyone in the world who might care to ask what I would be doing with my life,"[8] he explained. On his seventeenth birthday he joined the army.

The army was not what he imagined it would be. His three years of service coincided with the beginning of the Vietnam War (1955–1975), and his time in Vietnam was spent training South Vietnamese officers. He described those years as "numbing years. Years of learning to kill efficiently. Years of teaching others to kill efficiently. Years of nongrowing."[9] Then, a few years after he returned home, his brother Sonny also joined the army and was killed in Vietnam on his first day of combat. Myers was devastated—especially because he knew Sonny had enlisted because he admired Myers and was trying to follow in his footsteps.

Discovering His Purpose

After he finished his service in the army, Myers drifted. He was no longer writing, and he had no idea what he wanted to do with the rest of his life. He was also drinking heavily. For the next few years, he moved from one low-paying job to another, until one day, while working construction, he had an epiphany. Covered with the dirt and dust from demolition work, he was sitting on the curb when a pretty woman passed by and gave him a look of disgust. On the spot, he decided that he needed to start writing again. "I didn't need to get published, or to make money from my writing; I just needed to be able to think of myself as a person with a brain as well as a body,"[10] he said.

Once Myers started writing again, he found the purpose and personal identity he had been missing. Over the next several years he submitted poems, short stories, and articles to literary magazines and got a few published. Then, he came across a short story called "Sonny's Blues" by the African American writer James Baldwin. Baldwin had grown up a few blocks away from where Myers had lived in Harlem, and the story is about the experiences of the young black men who lived there. It was the first time that Myers realized that great literature could be about the black urban experience. "By humanizing the people who were like me, Baldwin's story . . . gave me a permission that I didn't know I needed," he explained, "the permission to write about my own landscape, my own map."[11]

A Distinguished Career

Once Myers began to draw from his own life in his writing, he started publishing regularly. He also began to seek out other African American writers, joined the Harlem Writer's Guild, and took classes in creative writing. One of his mentors recommended him for a job at the publishing house Bobbs-Merrill, and he was hired

A Speech Impediment

When Walter started elementary school, he discovered that he did not talk like the other children; he had a speech impediment. Because of this, he was teased at school, especially when he had to read in front of the class. Walter usually retaliated by hitting the child who had teased him—which meant that he spent a lot of time in punishment in the back of the room.

One day, his fifth-grade teacher caught him reading a comic book during his punishment and gave him a book of Norwegian fairy tales to read instead. "It was the best book I had ever read," he remembers. According to Myers, that book put him on the path to becoming a reader and a writer. "Reading . . . was like discovering a different language," he explains. "It was a language clearer than the one I spoke, and clearer than the one I heard around me. . . . The 'me' who read the books . . . seemed more the real me than the 'me' who played ball in the streets."

Inspired by his newfound love of reading, Walter started writing. He quickly discovered that if he wrote his own poems and stories, he could read them more easily in front of the class. His teachers were impressed by his writing and encouraged him to continue. It soon became obvious that the child whom the other children called a "dummy" was an intelligent student and a talented writer.

Walter Dean Myers, *Bad Boy*. New York: HarperCollins, 2001. Kindle edition.

as an acquisitions editor. During this time he married his first wife, Joyce, and had two children, Karen and Michael. Their marriage later dissolved.

In 1968 Myers won first prize in a contest sponsored by the Council on Interracial Books for Children for a children's picture book, which was published the next year as *Where Does the Day Go?* He continued to publish picture books in the early 1970s, and by the mid-1970s he had branched out to young adult novels. In 1973 he married his second wife, Constance, who gave birth to his son Christopher in 1974.

Then, in 1977 Myers was laid off from Bobbs-Merrill. Constance suggested he try to make a living by writing full time, and he agreed. He began a rigorous writing routine, waking up at five a.m. and writing five pages a day, five days a week. That schedule allowed him to publish more than a hundred books for young people, which included fiction, historical nonfiction, biographies, children's picture books, and collections of poetry. Over the span of his career his books for young people won nearly every award available in the genre, and he was a three-time finalist for the National Book Award for Young People's Literature.

Giving Children of Color a Voice

Throughout his writing career, Myers had a personal mission: to write the stories of the children of color who were not represented in literature. One of his most celebrated novels is *Monster* (1999), which has been compared to classics in young adult literature such as J.D. Salinger's *Catcher in the Rye* and S.E. Hinton's *The Outsiders* and is frequently taught in high school English classes. *Monster* is the story of sixteen-year-old Steve Harmon, an African American boy on trial for murder. Steve is accused of acting as a lookout for the burglary of a corner store, which results in the shop owner being shot and killed by the other two men on trial. The innovative novel is written partially in the form of a screenplay that Steve, who is a film student, writes while in jail during his trial. The novel explores the nature of truth: if Steve did act as a lookout, is he really a "monster," as the prosecution suggests, or is he a good kid who simply made a terrible mistake? It also portrays the terror that many young African Americans feel in prison. To research the novel, Myers drew on his experience tutoring and counseling young people in juvenile detention. *Monster* has won the most awards of any of Myers's books, including the Coretta Scott King Award and Michael L. Printz Award.

Another novel that is frequently assigned in high school English classes is *Fallen Angels* (1988), an antiwar story about young black soldiers in Vietnam. Myers wrote the book as a way to process his feelings about his own experiences in Vietnam and his brother Sonny's death there. The story is about Richie Perry,

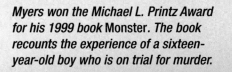

a seventeen-year-old boy who, like Myers, enlists in the army to escape his life in Harlem. Richie thinks that the war will be an adventure, but he soon learns how horrible war can be—especially for young black men, who were often given the most dangerous assignments.

The book is both realistic and graphic—the soldiers use profanity, and both soldiers and civilians die violent deaths. For this reason, the novel has been banned from many school libraries. However, most critics agree that it raises important issues about the realities of war, realities that Myers had experienced firsthand

and that he wished that he and his brother had understood before they enlisted. "Learning about wars has the power, I believe, to stop wars," Myers said. "Teenagers who read the book in the seventh grade eventually become the decision makers who send or don't send soldiers out to war. They begin to understand the demands of combat and the stresses which are involved."[12] Myers was so passionate about educating young people about war that he later wrote two more war novels: *Sunrise over Fallujah* (2008), which is about the conflict in Iraq, and the World War II novel *Invasion* (2013).

Because of his commitment to representing African American young people in literature, in 2012 the Library of Congress and the Children's Book Council named Myers the National Ambassador for Young People's Literature. He continued to promote diversity in children's literature right up until his death in 2014. In an

Timeless Appeal

Even though Walter Dean Myers's career spanned forty-five years, his books still seem fresh and current to young readers. To achieve this, Myers avoided putting slang in his work—in part because slang terms go in and out of fashion so quickly. "Mostly I try to stay in tune with how young people are feeling," he said. "If I can hook into that, capture those feelings and fears, then I'm usually okay. Also, I like making up my own 'today's' expressions."

Another reason his books still appeal to kids today is that they are full of action. When Myers outlined his stories he made sure that each and every scene had something physical going on in it. His writing style is also simple and straightforward, which draws kids in—even those who struggle with reading. In 2012, eighth grader Gaelyn Smith said of Myers's writing, "His books are real. They're not contrived at all. There's no generational barrier. That he's able to do that is amazing."

Walter Dean Myers, "Walter Dean Myers," *Interviewly*, December 2013. http://interviewly.com.

Quoted in Neely Tucker, "Walter Dean Myers: Bad Boy Makes Good," *Washington Post*, January 20, 2012. www.washingtonpost.com.

essay he wrote that year for the *New York Times*, he said, "Books transmit values. They explore our common humanity. What is the message when some children are not represented in those books? . . . Where are black children going to get a sense of who they are and what they can be?"[13]

Myers passed away on July 1, 2014, after a short illness. He was seventy-six years old. His son Christopher believed that literature was one of the most important things in his father's life and that books had given Myers both a sense of identity and a way to change the world. According to Christopher, his father "felt that he owed books a repayment. All his books were about rendering the invisible visible."[14]

> "All his books were about rendering the invisible visible."[14]
>
> —Christopher Myers

CHAPTER 2

J.K. Rowling

J.K. Rowling has been credited with ushering in a new golden age of young adult literature. Her *Harry Potter* books, published between 1997 and 2007, have sold more than 450 million copies worldwide, making Rowling the first billionaire author in history. Rowling's award-winning books were the first to appeal to both children and adults on a massive scale. In fact, they dominated the adult hardcover best-seller list for so many weeks that the *New York Times* created a separate list for young adult fiction.

In many ways, the story of how Rowling wrote and published the *Harry Potter* books is as magical as the world she created in her best-selling novels. In a few short years, Rowling went from being a single mother on welfare to breaking publishing records. Reserved by nature, Rowling has gradually adjusted to her fame and fortune, but she insists that she will never forget how far she has come.

A "Not Especially Fascinating" Childhood

Joanne Rowling was born on July 31, 1965, in the town of Chipping Sodbury, a suburb of Bristol, England. She took to writing at a very young age, finishing her first "book" when she was six—a story about a rabbit named Rabbit who gets sick with the measles, which she read to her younger sister, Dianne. In an autobiographical essay titled, "The Not Especially Fascinating Life So Far of J.K. Rowling," she writes, "Ever since Rabbit . . . I have wanted to be a writer, though I rarely told anyone so. I was afraid they'd tell me I didn't have a hope."[15]

When Joanne was nine, her family moved to a cottage in the nearby village of Tutshill, a rural area full of fields and forests. Her years in Tutshill were not particularly happy. She had a difficult relationship with her father and was alternately afraid of him and eager for his approval. When Rowling was fifteen, her mother was diagnosed with multiple sclerosis—a disease of the nervous system that at the time had no treatment—which put an enormous strain on the Rowlings. Along with these family difficulties, Joanne felt out of place in the rural setting. And though she had friends, and has many good memories from those years, she was also bullied and teased by her classmates and was insecure about almost everything. "Being a teenager can be completely horrible,"[16] she states.

She attended Wyedean School in Tutshill, where she did well; in her senior year she was named "head girl," the British equivalent of valedictorian. Although few Wyedean students went on to college, Rowling attended Exeter College in Oxford. She had never lost her interest in writing, but her mother had encouraged her to study French instead so she could work as a translator. She graduated from Exeter with a degree in French and classics in 1986.

Imagining Harry Potter

For the next few years Rowling worked at a series of jobs in London, most notably as a bilingual secretary for Amnesty International, a human rights organization. Then, in 1990, on a delayed train trip from Manchester to London, she got the idea for Harry Potter. She remembers that the idea began with an image of Harry—a scrawny, bespectacled boy of about eleven moving through an old-fashioned train coach. "I've never felt that excited about anything to do with

J.K. Rowling presents the seventh and final Harry Potter *book to fans in 2007. Rowling's imaginative series about a boy wizard has sold more than 450 million copies worldwide.*

writing," she remembers. "It was that incredibly elated feeling you get when you've just met someone with whom you might eventually fall in love."[17] She began to construct the story during the train ride: Harry, who is an orphan, discovers that there is a secret world of magic that exists alongside the normal world. He learns that he has magical powers and attends Hogwarts School of Witchcraft and Wizardry, a boarding school that trains young witches and wizards in the magical arts. The seven-part series follows his years at Hogwarts from his early training to his final confrontation with Lord

Voldemort, the evil wizard who killed his parents when Harry was a baby.

For the next few months, Rowling told no one about *Harry Potter*—not even her mother, who was at that time quite ill. Then, on December 30, 1990, her mother died from multiple sclerosis at only forty-five years old. Rowling was devastated. She deeply regrets never telling her mother about her plans for the books, which she believes her mother would have loved.

Her mother's death had a great impact on the development of Harry's story. "I really think from that moment on, death became a central, if not the central, theme of the seven books,"[18] Rowling explains. While she had always planned for Harry to be an orphan, after her own mother's death, Harry's feelings about his own mother—who had sacrificed herself to save him—became an important part of the story. She admits that she gave many of her own feelings about her mother's death to Harry, who gets to know his mother by talking to her in a magical mirror.

A Dark Time

After her mother's death, Rowling took a job teaching English as a second language in Portugal. There she met Jorge Arantes, a journalism student. The two were married, and in 1993 they had a daughter, Jessica. By then, Rowling's marriage to Arantes had collapsed. She returned to Britain with her infant daughter and settled in Edinburgh, Scotland. "I felt life was a train wreck," she remembers. "I'd carried this baby out of it, and I was in this place that was very alien and cold, and quite grim."[19]

The next few months were the darkest period of her life. By her own account, Rowling was as poor as a person could be and not be homeless. She applied for welfare and rented a cramped, dilapidated apartment. Her future seemed bleak and she slipped into depression. The one thing that gave her hope was her novel, so she decided to finish it. Slowly, Rowling pulled herself out of her dreary circumstances, and in 1995, she finished *Harry Potter and the Philosopher's Stone*.

> "I felt life was a train wreck."[19]
>
> —J.K. Rowling

Finding a Home for Harry

Rowling found a literary agent who believed in her book, but he advised her that it would be a tough sell. At the time, most books aimed at young adults were short novels (*Harry Potter and the Philosopher's Stone* is the length of a typical adult novel), mainly because publishers believed that children did not have the attention span to stay engaged with a longer book. In addition, the series itself follows a group of children who mature through seven years of school. Harry and his friends age from eleven to eighteen over the span of the series and deal with issues like puberty, first love, and personal identity. This was unlike most children's series of the time; characters tended not to age more than a year or two over the course of a series so that they would appeal to a consistent age group of readers.

Rowling's agent began submitting the novel to publishers. One by one, they rejected it. Finally, Nigel Newton, chairman at Bloomsbury Publishing in London, decided to take a chance on the book. When Rowling's agent called her with the good news, she was ecstatic. "I could not quite believe my ears," she remembers. "After I had hung up, I screamed and jumped into the air."[20]

Her editor asked her to use initials for her first name so that her gender would not be obvious. (At the time, many publishers believed that boys would be less likely to read a book if it was written by a woman.) As Rowling has no middle name, she chose the initial "K" for Kathleen, her grandmother's name.

A Literary Celebrity

Only about five hundred copies of *Harry Potter and the Philosopher's Stone* were printed initially, but it nonetheless began to receive rave reviews and awards, including the British Book Award and the Nestlé Smarties Book Prize. Then, Scholastic Publishing in the United States paid more than $100,000 for the American rights to the novel—an unheard-of sum for a children's book by a first-time novelist. (The novel was retitled *Harry Potter and the Sorcerer's Stone* for US publication.) Rowling had done

Publisher's Daughter Picks *Harry Potter*

When J.K. Rowling's agent, Christopher Little, submitted *Harry Potter and the Philosopher's Stone* to Bloomsbury Publishing, it had already been rejected by all of the major publishing houses in London. Bloomsbury, a small and relatively new company, was the novel's last chance at publication. Little gave a sample of the manuscript to Bloomsbury's chairman, Nigel Newton, who took it home but did not read it; instead, he handed it to his eight-year-old daughter, Alice.

Alice took the chapters upstairs, but soon was back, begging for more of the story. As Newton remembers, "She came down from her room an hour later glowing, saying, 'Dad, this is so much better than anything else.' She nagged and nagged me in the following months, wanting to see what came next."

That was all Newton needed to hear. He agreed to publish the book. "It was very fortunate for us," he said. "We'd only just started to publish children's books. . . . And we hit it lucky."

Quoted in John Lawless, "Revealed: The Eight-Year-Old Girl Who Saved Harry Potter," *New Zealand Herald News*, July 3, 2005. www.nzherald.co.nz.

what few novelists ever do—she had achieved financial success through her writing.

But nobody could have predicted the success of Rowling's *Harry Potter* books. By 1999, when books two and three of the series had been published, Rowling became the first author to have three books in the top three spots on the *New York Times* best-seller list at the same time. The fourth volume, *Harry Potter and the Goblet of Fire*, became the fastest-selling book in history. Its distribution (at one minute after midnight on its publication date) was accompanied by elaborate book release events that were attended by thousands of costumed fans—most of them children.

Rowling had reached celebrity status, something that she—and everyone else in the publishing industry—was entirely unprepared for. Minna Fry, a former marketing director at Bloomsbury, said that the entire team was stunned by the crowds at the book

Young fans—sporting Harry Potter–style hats and glasses—hold on to the first copies of the latest installment in the series. Midnight book release parties became a common occurrence, attended by thousands of mostly young, costumed fans.

release event for the publication of *Goblet of Fire*. "There were parents beating up other parents to get into the queue [the book-signing line],"[21] she remembers. Rowling was overwhelmed by her sudden fame. "It was like being a Beatle," she explains, referring to the famous musical group. "As a writer, I had no one near me, either professionally or personally, who could in any way help when I had questions like, 'What do you do when the press is searching your [trash] bins?' It took everyone around me totally by surprise. I was really running scared for a while."[22]

Christian Controversy

As the *Harry Potter* books gained popularity, some Christian groups became concerned that they carried the message that witchcraft was glamorous and fun and encouraged its practice among children. Because Rowling based the magic depicted in the books on pagan and occult literature and myth, these groups believed that much of the witchcraft in the stories was realistic and could open the door to real occult influences in their children's lives. For instance, the books detail spells, curses, and potion recipes; depict communicating with the spirit world and human sacrifice; and generally portray those without magical powers as lesser beings. In one scene that Christian critics claim is full of occultist imagery, Harry is tied to a gravestone and a shapeshifter, in the form of a rat, utters a death curse that kills his friend Cedric. According to Christian bookseller Clara Sessoms, "Anyone who knows anything about spiritual warfare knows those books can open the door to spiritual bondage. . . . And I think it's worse that children are the target."[23]

At the height of the controversy, several Christian groups protested the novels at book launch parties and even staged book-burning events. In addition, some Christian parents began to challenge whether the *Harry Potter* books should be included in their children's school libraries or on classroom reading lists. In 1999 alone, the books were challenged twenty-three times in the United States. The American Library Association has stated that the *Harry Potter* novels are the most challenged books of the current century.

> "Those books can open the door to spiritual bondage."[23]
>
> —Christian bookseller Clara Sessoms.

In 1999, award-winning children's author Judy Blume spoke out in the *New York Times* about these efforts to censor the books: "Some parents believe they have the right to demand immediate removal of any book for any reason from school or classroom libraries," she writes. "The list of gifted teachers and librarians who find their jobs in jeopardy for defending their students' right to read, to imagine, to question, grows every year."[24] Like Rowling, Blume believes that wizards and magic are part of our literary heritage and simply inspire in children a love of reading. And the *Harry Potter* books were inspiring children—as they grew in popularity, parents and teachers all over the world reported that children were suddenly interested in reading. As English teacher Lindsay Carmichael remembers, "I was teaching 10- and 11-year-olds when the first wave of Pottermania hit. . . . It was extraordinary—suddenly all my pupils were reading. Not only were the children interested, but they were excited and inspired by books."[25]

Saying Good-bye to Harry

After *Goblet of Fire* was published in 2000, Rowling remarried. She and her husband, Neil Murray, built a home in Scotland, where they had two children, David and Mackenzie. Rowling continued

The Casual Vacancy

J.K. Rowling's first adult novel, *The Casual Vacancy*, explores issues of class, politics, and poverty in the United Kingdom. The story focuses in part on sixteen-year-old Krystal Weedon, whose mother is a heroin-addicted prostitute who has trapped Krystal and her three-year-old brother in a cycle of poverty, drugs, and violence.

Social issues have always been important to Rowling, and she has spoken often about how dehumanizing it is to live in poverty. She has given millions to charities that fight poverty and support children's welfare. In fact, in 2012 *Forbes* reported that Rowling's total charitable donations topped $160 million.

Rowling spent five years writing *The Casual Vacancy*. She knew that the book would be under a great deal of scrutiny from the public, so to avoid being overwhelmed by the pressure to meet readers' expectations she told herself that she did not have to publish it unless she wanted to. She was pleased with the result, however, and the book was published in 2012. Although the novel was a financial success, reviews were mixed. Book critic Michiko Kakutani of the *New York Times* called the story "dull" and filled with "self-absorbed, small-minded, snobbish and judgmental folks, whose stories neither engage nor transport us." On the other hand, critic Lev Grossman of *Time* called it "a big, ambitious, brilliant, profane, funny, very upsetting and magnificently eloquent novel of contemporary England."

Michiko Kakutani, "Darkness and Death, No Magic to Help," *New York Times*, September 27, 2012. www.nytimes.com.

Lev Grossman, "J.K. Rowling's *The Casual Vacancy*: We've Read It, Here's What We Think," *Time*, September 27, 2012. http://time.com.

writing during this period. Each successive volume of the seven-part series broke sales records, and the final volume has been said to be the most anticipated book in publishing history.

On January 11, 2007, Rowling finished the final installment of the *Harry Potter* series, *Harry Potter and the Deathly Hallows*. She had been writing the *Harry Potter* books for seventeen years, and it was difficult to let the story go. "Initially I was elated," she says, "but then I cried as I've only ever done once before, and that was when my mother died. I knew I'd still be writing, but I had to mourn Harry."[26]

After Harry

After finishing the final *Harry Potter* book, Rowling turned her attention to adult novels. In 2012 she published *The Casual Vacancy*. She then wrote three crime novels, known as the *Cormoran Strike* series. Her adult novels have received mixed reviews, but all have been successful financially.

Though she has said that there will almost certainly be no more *Harry Potter* books, she has not abandoned Harry's world altogether. Information about the world of Harry Potter can be found on her website, *Pottermore*, and she has collaborated on a stage play, *Harry Potter and the Cursed Child*, scheduled to premiere in July 2016. And in 2015 Rowling announced that she is at work on another children's book. Like all of Rowling's projects, the topic of the book is a closely guarded secret. But no matter what it is about, her fans will surely find it magical.

CHAPTER 3

Nnedi Okorafor

Nnedi Okorafor is one of the few female writers of African descent working in the fantasy and science fiction field. Her young adult and adult fiction has won dozens of awards and has resonated with readers all over the world—especially girls, because she often gives her female characters magical powers that allow them to embrace their inner strength and rise above their circumstances.

But Okorafor is not just a fantastic storyteller; her fiction explores the complex environmental, cultural, and political issues of Africa. She fills her version of Africa with fantastical creatures and blends magic and technology in inventive and surprising ways. According to award-winning science fiction writer Ursula K. Le Guin, "There's more vivid imagination in a page of Nnedi Okorafor's work than in whole volumes of ordinary fantasy epics."[27]

Africa is Okorafor's muse, and she views it from a unique perspective. Born to Nigerian parents, Okorafor is an African American who has never really fit into any racial culture—and she is just fine with that.

American or Nigerian?

Nnedimma Nkemdili Okorafor was born on April 8, 1974, in Cincinnati, Ohio. Her parents came to the United States from Nigeria in 1969 to pursue their education and escape the Biafran War (the Nigerian civil war fought from 1967 to 1970). The Okorafors were the first black family to live in the town of South Holland, Illinois, and in the 1980s, Nnedi experienced a lot of blatant racism. "I used to fight a lot as a kid, and there was one boy I [slapped] after he called me a n——. He deserved it."[28] Later, when the family moved to Olympia Springs, Illinois, Nnedi experienced another kind of racism—from African Americans who discriminated against the family for "acting white." "I was sort of outcast in multiple communities," she explains. "So I grew up with little interest in 'fitting in.' I just did my thing. And I'm still doing that."[29]

Though Nnedi's parents were naturalized American citizens, their Nigerian roots were very important to them. Beginning when Nnedi was seven years old, they began to take her and her two older sisters (and later her younger brother) to Nigeria to visit family and experience Nigerian culture. These experiences were very helpful to young Nnedi. In Nigeria, she encountered a world where her race was not nearly as important as it was in the United

Biafran refugees flee Nigerian troops in 1968, during the civil war. Nnedi Okorafor was born in the United States to parents who had fled the war-torn country in 1969.

States. She remembers that the trips were "really eye opening and fun" and "very, very nurturing."[30] These visits instilled in her a sense of dual identity: American and Nigerian. She also developed a deep love of Africa, which became the inspiration for the futuristic settings of most of her young adult fiction.

A Voracious Reader

When Nnedi was a young girl, reading was one of her favorite pastimes. She was not especially drawn to science fiction and fantasy, the genres in which she would later write. Instead, she tended to ignore categories and chose whatever caught her eye in the library. Many of these books were written for adults, not children. "I read a lot of books that I definitely had no business reading at that age,"[31] she says. By age twelve, she had become especially fond of the horror writer Stephen King, whom she cites as a strong influence on her later writing.

> "I read a lot of books that I definitely had no business reading."[31]
>
> —Nnedi Okorafor

When Nnedi did read science fiction, she had a difficult time connecting with the characters and situations. Science fiction tends to be written by and populated with white people, and Nnedi did not see herself, her family, or her African heritage reflected in those stories. "I felt more like a tourist in those stories than a citizen,"[32] she explains. This is one reason she populates her own books with people of color—so that children who are not normally represented in speculative fiction can see themselves in her stories.

A Budding Scientist and Athlete

Even though Nnedi loved to read, as a child she had no aspirations to become a writer. "I loved them [stories]. Just the idea of just disappearing into a story was a natural thing for me," she says. "But I never thought to try to write a story myself."[33] Her parents valued math and science more highly than artistic pursuits— her father was a heart surgeon, and her mother had earned her PhD in medical administration—and Nnedi was especially good

Surgery Gone Wrong

Though Okorafor was athletic as a child, she also had scoliosis—a disorder of the spinal column in which the spine develops an abnormal, side-to-side curvature. She underwent surgery for the condition after her freshman year of college. When she awoke after surgery, she was horrified to discover that she was paralyzed from the waist down. Her doctors were not sure what was causing the paralysis, but they feared that her spinal cord may have been damaged during the surgery. Okorafor was terrified—especially since the doctors could not tell her whether she would ever walk again.

Over that summer, Okorafor used the same determination and discipline that had made her an accomplished athlete to relearn how to walk—first with a walker and then with a cane. When she returned to college in the fall, she was unsteady on her feet and still needed a cane to help balance herself.

She credits her recuperation from spinal surgery as the reason she became a writer. "When I was sitting in that bed, just devastated and scared and all of that, that's when I started writing," she remembers. "They often say . . . a traumatic experience kicks [artists] into motion. That was my traumatic experience."

Nnedi Okorafor, interviewed by Sarah Culberson, "Nnedi Okorafor on the Africa Channel's 'Behind the Words' Part 1," YouTube, December 29, 2010. www.youtube.com/watch?v=Vboc3UVVTk8.

at math and science in school. She was also drawn to the natural world. "Living in the suburbs of Chicago gave me lots of space and a lot of empty weed-filled lots to explore," she recalls. "It's in these empty lots, forest preserves and nature centers that I cultivated my love for flora and fauna."[34] Because of her deep love of nature and her facility with math and science, she seemed to be on the path to become a biologist. She especially loved bugs and liked the idea of becoming an entomologist, a biologist who studies insects.

Nnedi was also athletic and good at sports; she was always picked first for games when her friends were choosing up teams on the playground. She was especially talented at track and field and at tennis, and at nine years old she began to play tennis at the semiprofessional level. From then until her first year of college, she defined herself as an athlete. "Up to the age of 19, my life revolved around two things," she says. "Sports and books."[35]

Discovering a Love of Writing

The summer after Okorafor's freshman year of college, she underwent surgery to correct an abnormality in her spine. Due to serious complications her recuperation took longer than expected, and she found herself confined to bed for much of the summer. It was then that she started writing for the first time. When she returned to college, her boyfriend suggested she take a creative writing class. The class was a revelation, she says: "Once I wrote my very first story . . . I never stopped writing from that point on. I realized that this was what I love doing."[36] By the end of that semester, she had started writing a novel.

Okorafor continued to write one novel after another during college, with no thought to pursuing publication. She earned a degree in rhetoric from the University of Illinois in 1996 and went on to earn a master of arts degree in journalism from Michigan State University in 1999. At that point, she was considering pursuing a career in journalism. But creative writing still pulled at her.

Finding Her Calling

Okorafor credits her decision to pursue creative writing to a twist of fate. After earning her master's degree in journalism, she was not sure whether she wanted to be a reporter or a fiction writer. To help her decide, she applied to two programs: the Clarion Workshop, a six-week writing workshop for aspiring science fiction and fantasy writers, and a competitive journalism internship at the *Chicago Sun-Times*. Even though she went through a grueling interview process for the internship, she never heard back from the *Sun-Times*. Clarion, however, accepted her, and she attended Clarion East in 2001.

The workshop was an eye-opening experience for Okorafor. Before the workshop, she had not identified herself as a fantasy/science fiction writer. Although her writing was highly imaginative, her creative writing classes in college had tended to be dismissive of writing that was not realistic. But when she arrived at Clarion, she realized that speculative genres like fantasy and science fiction could—and should—be taught and critiqued with the same rigor and seriousness as other types of fiction. She also

At one point in her life, Okorafor was trying to decide whether to become a news reporter or pursue creative writing. After her acceptance to a writer's workshop, she chose fiction writing.

felt right at home with the other writers at Clarion. "I thought, 'Oh, these are my people!'" she says. "'These are who I belong with, and this is what I am.'"[37]

After her experience at Clarion, Okorafor decided to pursue fiction writing as a career. Because her family put such an emphasis on education, she earned a PhD in creative writing from the University of Chicago in 2007. By this time she had given birth to a daughter, Anyaugo, and had published her first young adult novel, *Zahrah the Windseeker* in 2005.

Fantasy with African Roots

Okorafor first became known for her ability to weave elements of Africa into her speculative fiction with *Zahrah the Windseeker*. The novel is about a girl named Zahrah who is born on a faraway planet called Ginen, a world where technology is plant based

The Magical Negro

Okorafor is not only a fiction writer; she is also a professor of literature, and she writes and lectures about the ways that literature intersects with society. In one of her noted essays, she tackles a stereotypical character in fiction known as the "Magical Negro." This African American character is benevolent and wise, has magical powers, and helps a story's white protagonist—often through self-sacrifice. In her essay "Stephen King's Super-Duper Magical Negroes," Okorafor criticizes King for using this character frequently in his fiction. She writes: "The grand result of the repeated use of the Magical Negro archetype . . . is the implication that black people are inferior and expendable, even when they have power to wield, and white people are superior and important, even when they have to rely on the Magical Negro."

On the other hand, Okorafor acknowledges that King's Magical Negroes are some of the best characters he has ever written. As a writer, she knows that the character type is an agent of change, and that when one shows up, "the story crackles and pops." Despite her concerns about racism inherent in King's Magical Negro characters, King is one of her favorite authors. "King is *not* a racist," she insists.

Nnedi Okorafor-Mbachu, "Stephen King's Super-Duper Magical Negroes," *Strange Horizons*, October 25, 2004. www.strangehorizons.com.

and everything—from buildings to computers—is grown. Like many young adult novels, *Zahrah the Windseeker* is about finding strength in being different, but in imagining those differences, Okorafor drew from the myths and folklore of Africa. In the story, Zahrah is born "dada"—a West African term that means that a baby is born with unusually rough and curly hair that cannot be combed; in Zahrah's case, her hair also harbors strange vines. In West Africa, some people believe that being born dada means that a child has special powers given to him or her by evil spirits, and dada children are sometimes shunned or feared. Zahrah also faces this prejudice in her world and is bullied by the other children. But when she is thirteen, she discovers that her dadalocks give her the power of flight, which she uses to try to save her only friend. Stories of people who can fly are prevalent in African mythology, and Zahrah's power of flight as a "windseeker" becomes a central plot device in the book.

Like all of Okorafor's fantasy novels, *Zahrah the Windseeker* is also filled with strange and magical creatures; in the jungles of Ginen, there are talking frogs, horse-eating birds, and spiders the size of small children. Okorafor bases many of these creatures on animals she has encountered in Nigeria. "Whenever I visit Nigeria, you can bet that I will witness wonders," she says. "Spiders flat as paper or huge as a king crab. Indestructible wasps. A monkey sitting on the side of the road like an old woman. Rainbow colored grasshoppers. Immortal cockroaches. Disappearing wall geckos. I can go on and on. These things always hiding in the nooks and crannies of my novels."[38]

In 2008, *Zahrah the Windseeker* was awarded the Wole Soyinka Prize for Literature in Africa, in part because the novel takes elements of African culture and myth and reimagines them in a positive way—something Okorafor sees as one of her missions as a fiction writer. Winning the award was a pivotal event for Okorafor, who said it made her feel "truly recognized as a novelist"[39] for the first time. Noted critic Gary Wolfe of *Locus Magazine* calls the novel "a consistently compelling and provocative tale that suggests new ways of treating folkloristic material, particularly African folklore, in a science-fictional setting."[40]

Okorafor published her second young adult novel, *The Shadow Speaker*, in 2008. The novel had been her doctoral dissertation and received positive reviews. She then started teaching at Chicago State University and continued to publish award-winning novels and short stories for both young people and adults. Eventually, she took a position at the University of Buffalo, where she is currently a professor of creative writing and literature. She says she loves teaching because it gives her life balance. "If I had the time to . . . write all the time, I know I would,"[41] she admits.

> "If I had the time to . . . write all the time, I know I would."[41]
>
> —Nnedi Okorafor

Tackling a Controversial Issue

Because Okorafor does not feel that she fits into any culture or tradition, she often examines the traditions of Africa as an outsider—an American of Nigerian descent attempting to understand her roots. In Okorafor's opinion, the best way to do this is to write from the point of view of an insider—a person who participates in a particular tradition. Her portrayal of the controversial practice of female circumcision, a procedure in which a young girl's clitoris is removed, in her adult novel *Who Fears Death* (2010) is an example of how writing from an insider's point of view caused controversy among some in the African community.

Who Fears Death is about a girl named Onyesonwu, a child of rape born in a post-apocalyptic Africa. Because her mother was raped, she is not accepted by her culture. In an attempt to fit in with her people, she willingly submits to a ritual that mirrors the real practice of female circumcision, also known as genital mutilation. Okorafor herself is horrified by the practice, which is still performed in some African cultures. But in *Who Fears Death*, she wanted to examine some of the reasons why women might submit to it.

Okorafor was criticized for the way she portrayed the ritual and Onyesonwu's feelings about it. "I had feminists who were angry with me for portraying the ritual sympathetically," she says. "Some people said I was pro-female-genital mutilation."[42] She also was criticized by other African writers and academics, who thought that by describing such a horrific practice Okorafor was casting African people in a negative light. But Okorafor had her own reasons for showing why her character chose to be circumcised; she wanted readers who condoned the practice to relate to Onyesonwu, who later deeply regrets what she has done. "You can't just tell people they're bad, because they're never going to listen to you,"[43] she explains. Okorafor hoped that showing how the ritual harms a girl's sense of self and reduces her power in the world would lead more people to reject the practice.

Empowering Girls of Color

An extremely prolific writer, Okorafor has written many other works of young adult fiction, including *The Akata Witch* (2011) and *Akata Witch 2: Breaking Kola* (2016). Her adult novels include *Lagoon* (2014) and *The Book of Phoenix* (2015). She has also written children's books, short stories and novellas, scholarly essays, plays, and screenplays. Her young adult fiction continues to reimagine Africa and to represent the young people who live there, showing them a future where the power of girls and young women of color makes a difference.

CHAPTER 4

Rainbow Rowell

ainbow Rowell is a romantic. "I *love* love stories," she explains. "They're my favorite thing about every story."[44] Falling in love, staying in love, fighting for love in the face of overwhelming obstacles—these are the themes that Rowell explores in her novels. Her characters are not the typical heroes and heroines that populate young adult fiction: the girls are plus-sized, the boys are awkward and nerdy—and the wizards are gay. Regardless, however, of whether her novels feature teenagers or adults, or are rooted in realism or fantasy, at their core is a meticulously drawn, emotionally honest love story. As young adult author Leigh Bardugo states, "Rainbow writes falling in love like nobody's business."[45]

> "Rainbow writes falling in love like nobody's business."[45]
>
> —Leigh Bardugo, young adult author.

A Difficult Childhood

Rainbow Rowell was born on February 24, 1973, in Omaha, Nebraska. She grew up in extreme poverty; her family moved from place to place in and around the city of Omaha, and at times they did not have a car, a phone, electricity, or even running

Rainbow Rowell spent most of her young life in and around Omaha, Nebraska (pictured). At times her family lived without a car, a phone, electricity, or running water.

water. Growing up poor had a huge impact on young Rainbow. "When you are that poor, it's present in your every moment and interaction," she explains. "That poverty is a huge part of who you are in every moment."[46]

Her father, an army veteran, was rarely around, and he left the family when Rainbow was in the second grade. Though she does have fond memories of her father reading C.S. Lewis's *The Lion, the Witch, and the Wardrobe* to her and her siblings, her relationship with her father was, as she puts it, "not good. There was a lot of alcohol abuse and drug abuse. . . . I'm probably sane and alive because I had a really great mom."[47]

An Early Reader and Writer

Rainbow's mother is an evangelical Christian, and she allowed Rainbow and her four siblings to watch very little television. However, the kids were allowed to read anything they wanted, and Rainbow quickly became a voracious reader. She would read during class, sneaking peeks at a book in her desk, and she would stay up all night reading by the bathroom light. She immersed herself first in children's authors such as Beverly Cleary and Louisa May Alcott and later in science fiction and fantasy novels. Reading gave Rainbow hope when she felt hopeless. "Even the prospect of reading gave me hope," she says. "Like, getting to read a book that I loved was enough to live for."[48]

She also discovered at a young age that she had a talent for writing. After a class trip to the zoo, Rainbow wrote a poem about gorillas watching soap operas for an assignment. "My teacher made a big deal about it,"[49] she remembers. Because of this early encouragement, her writing became a source of confidence and pride—one of the few things that she knew she could do well. Still, Rainbow did not imagine that she could ever be an author. Books were magical, and the thought of writing one seemed out of reach. Instead, she wanted to be a librarian, imagining spending her days stamping books with due dates and telling other people what to read.

> "I'm probably sane and alive because I had a really great mom."[47]
>
> —Rainbow Rowell

Teenage Struggles

Junior high and high school were the hardest years of Rainbow's life. She suffered from social anxiety, and she was overweight and uncomfortable with her appearance. "When I was younger, I believed in—and yearned for—conventional beauty," she recalls. "I thought that some features were universally attractive, and others were universally repulsive. And that fat was the worst of the worst. . . . Fat was what made you unlovable."[50] These issues, coupled with being poor, would have been difficult for any young person to deal with. But Rainbow had more serious problems at home. "As a teenager, I had a really bad stepdad," she admits. "I felt trapped and suffocated by the circumstances of my life."[51] (Rowell's mother has since remarried.)

The only way she could escape these circumstances was by losing herself in fictional worlds. Her love of fantasy and science fiction grew during this time, and in the seventh grade, she began to play Dungeons & Dragons, a fantasy role-playing game, after school. Also, like the protagonist in her second novel, *Eleanor & Park*, she became interested in comic books and would swap them with a friend on the school bus. At the time she wrote only fiction that continued the stories that she read in novels and comics—stories that featured super powers and love triangles—usually with herself as the romantic lead. These stories would now be considered fan fiction (new stories about characters created by another author), a genre that would later become the subject of her novel *Fangirl*. She also continued to read widely and deeply, as she explains: "I feel like books were the greatest gift I had. . . . Those years were about disappearing and going to a place where I could just be myself."[52]

Security in Journalism

Though Rainbow wrote fiction only for herself during these years, she had by now decided she wanted to write for a living and set her sights on becoming a journalist—a profession that would give her the financial security she had not had as a young person. She took journalism classes in high school and became involved in her school's newspaper. After high school she attended the University of Nebraska and worked on the college paper, the *Daily Nebraskan*. She graduated in 1995 with a triple major in English, journalism, and advertising. After college she married her boyfriend, Kai, who was a close friend from her days playing Dungeons & Dragons in junior high school.

Rowell started her career in journalism as an intern at the *Omaha World Herald*; later she worked as reporter, specializing in human interest stories. Her writing, as well as her knack for reporting quirky stories, led to a promotion: At only twenty-four, she became the youngest ever—as well as the first female—columnist at the *Herald*. For the next ten years, Rowell honed her writer's voice through her columns, developing what Shreeja Ravindranathan at *Friday Magazine* later described as a mix-

Why Rainbow?

One question that Rowell is frequently asked is whether or not Rainbow is her real name or a pen name. Rainbow is her real name. Her mother chose unusual names for most of her children—Rainbow's siblings are named Forest, Jade, Haven, and Jerry (she jokes that Jerry is the one with the weird name). Rowell admits there are positives and negatives to having such an unusual name. "People think I chose it myself, and then they wonder what sort of person would choose a name like 'Rainbow'"—which she claims is the sort of name a child would give her stuffed unicorn. But ultimately she believes the positives outweigh the negatives, explaining, "Growing up with a weird name kind of gave me permission to be different from my peers, if I wanted to be. When your name is 'Rainbow,' you never get to blend into the crowd."

Quoted in "Interview with Rainbow Rowell," Goodreads, December 2013. www.goodreads.com.

ture of "observational sharp humour, popular culture references and personal reflection that make her books so memorable and honest."[53]

Finding Success Writing for Herself

After a decade at the *Herald*, Rowell became dissatisfied with her job. "I felt like I couldn't grow up at that job, like I'd always be the kid,"[54] she explains. She also began to chafe at the restrictions writing for a conservative newspaper put on her creativity—and her sense of humor. She left the *Herald* for a job in advertising and began to write her first novel, *Attachments*, an adult romantic comedy set in a newsroom in 1999, when e-mail was first being used in workplaces. At first Rowell wrote only a series of e-mail exchanges between two of the female characters. She never intended to try to publish the book: "My only goal was to crack myself up," she explains. Rowell worked on the novel off and on for a few years, and when she and her husband decided to have children, she abandoned the book altogether. Two years later, her sister convinced her to finish it and find an agent. *Attachments* was published in 2011 and was named by *Kirkus Reviews* as one of the Outstanding Debuts of 2011.

Rowell's second novel, *Eleanor & Park*, established her as an award-winning young adult author. Published in 2013, it quickly became a *New York Times* best seller and has received a great deal of critical acclaim, including being named a 2014 Printz Honor book for young adult fiction. Rowell acknowledges that the story is somewhat autobiographical—Eleanor is an overweight girl who lives in poverty and has an abusive stepfather. But it is also an unconventional love story between a larger white girl and a smaller Korean boy. And it is the way Rowell's characters handle the obstacles they face that makes *Eleanor & Park* stand out. As young adult author John Green (*The Fault in Our Stars*) explains in his glowing review of the book, "The world cannot allow Eleanor a boyfriend of any kind, because she's poor and fat and dresses funny. The world cannot allow Park a girlfriend because he likes wearing eyeliner, and everyone knows that's gay. The world is the obstacle, as it always is when you're 16 and truly in love."[55] Rowell hoped that the book carried the message that "there are no rules in love and attraction—except for the ones you make with the person you choose and who chooses you."[56]

> "There are no rules in love and attraction."[56]
>
> —Rainbow Rowell

Eleanor & Park Controversy

Though *Eleanor & Park* is widely praised as a realistic account of the challenges teens can face on a day-to-day basis, a small group of parents in Minneapolis deemed the book "dangerously obscene"[57] and challenged the Anoka-Hennepin School District to remove it from public and school libraries and discipline those who had recommended it for a summer reading list. The group claimed that "this book is littered with extreme profanity and age-inappropriate subject matter that should never be put into the hands and minds of minor children"[58] and convinced the Anoka County Public Library to cancel an appearance by Rowell.

The controversy stunned Rowell, who insisted that there is no explicit sex in the book and that almost all of the profanity and sexual comments come from those bullying the main characters—a daily reality for many teens. She was also concerned that her visit was canceled. "It's so dangerous to keep ideas out of the public library just because you find them unpleasant or disagree with them," she explains. "The freedom to read is the freedom to think."[59]

The controversy received national attention; Linda Holmes, who writes NPR's entertainment and pop-culture blog, *Monkey See*, explains that banning *Eleanor & Park* sends the wrong message to teens. She says, "What's worrying about treating *Eleanor & Park* as a nasty book, or a dirty book, or an immoral book, is that it transforms talking about how to survive ugliness into something that's no different from ugliness itself."[60] The National Coalition Against Censorship also came to the defense of the book, as did Julie Blaha, president of the Anoka-Hennepin teachers union. She stated that *Eleanor & Park* is "a story about two students who fall in love, make the right choices and beat the odds. They rise above bullies, poverty and domestic abuse. To ignore that is to ignore a powerful, positive message for every teen who ever felt awkward or isolated in high school."[61]

The controversy, which ironically occurred during Banned Books Week (an annual event in which libraries draw attention to banned books and the problems of censorship) was ultimately settled by the school district, which decided that *Eleanor & Park* was "powerful, realistic and appropriate for high schoolers"[62] and decided to keep the book on library shelves.

Fan Fiction

Rowell continued to explore young adult issues with her next book, *Fangirl*. *Fangirl*'s protagonist is a college freshman named Cath who writes fan fiction about the fictional character Simon Snow—a teenage wizard of Rowell's creation who has deliberate similarities to J.K. Rowling's Harry Potter. Rowell is a huge fan of the *Harry Potter* novels and of the fan fiction that has sprung up around them. "I've always been a very fannish person," she says. "If I like something, I probably love it, and if I love it, I can't get enough."[63] She got the idea for *Fangirl* by wondering what her life as a teenager would have been like if the Internet-based fan community had existed in the 1980s.

One theme that *Fangirl* deals with is the way fan fiction—which is often written by women and girls—is often put down. "Anything that teenage girls do to express their romantic, or even sexual, feelings is automatically awful and shameful and something that shouldn't be talked about,"[64] Rowell says. In the novel, Cath writes Simon Snow fan fiction for a creative writing class. Her teacher claims that fan fiction is plagiarism, forcing Cath to choose between writing what she cares about and writing what is expected of her.

Rowell became so interested in Cath's fan fiction that she wrote the young adult fantasy novel *Carry On*, which explores the burgeoning romance between Simon and another young male wizard, Baz. While Rowell notes that the two are an unusual couple for the mainstream fantasy genre, she believes that there are already enough stories that hint at sexual attraction between

Rowell explores themes of love—falling in love, staying in love, and fighting for love—in her novels. Though she writes somewhat unconventional love stories, they are powerful and filled with passion.

NaNoWriMo

In November 2011, with two books under her belt, Rowell decided to participate in National Novel Writing Month (NaNoWriMo)—an Internet-based event that challenges writers to produce fifty thousand words in a single month. She used the event to write part of the first draft of her novel *Fangirl*. While she was not sure that she would produce anything of quality, the experience was a good one. "During that month, I tried to write 2,000 words a day. And I didn't let myself go back to reread or edit; the rule was that I had to start wherever I left off and push forward. It was tough." However, the experiment paid off, and Rowell was pleasantly surprised by the quality of what she produced. She also liked the way it focused her. "I stayed inside the story in a way I never had before; I stayed immersed. And I was looser and braver than normal," she explains. The experience was so positive that Rowell has continued writing in NaNoWriMo-style ever since.

Quoted in Julie Bartel, "One Thing Leads to Another: An Interview with Rainbow Rowell," *Hub,* February 27, 2014. www.yalsa.ala.org.

male friends (she cites the BBC television show *Sherlock*) and that young people want to read about real romance. Although *Carry On* is about more than just two male wizards falling in love, the romance is still the emotional core of the story. "I wouldn't have wanted to write it if they didn't fall in love,"[65] Rowell says.

Current Projects

Rowell is currently working on a screenplay for *Eleanor & Park*, which was picked up by the movie production company Dream-Works. She also has a two-book deal to write graphic novels, a project that draws on her love of comic books. When asked if she will concentrate on young adult or adult fiction going forward, she says that she simply tells the story she wants to tell. Rowell sees very little difference between books that are labeled young adult and those that are geared toward adults. "I don't think YA books are less sophisticated or not as well-written," she says. "There's as much diversity in quality among adult books as you'll find in YA."[66] But she does believe young adult readers—whether they are teens or adults—are "the most passionate readers there are."[67]

CHAPTER 5

John Green

John Green's novels are populated with smart, funny, eccentric teens who long for connection and community. But Green does more than just write stories that reflect these needs; he has created that community in the real world. Green's experiences as an outcast in middle school inspired him to create an online gathering place where young people can support and champion each other. A best-selling author with a huge online presence, Green has given voice to the big questions about life, love, and friendship that all teens grapple with.

A Lonely Childhood

John Michael Green was born on August 24, 1977, in Indianapolis, Indiana. His parents, Mike and Sydney Green, were devoted to John and his younger brother, Hank. Of his childhood, Green says, "I was extremely fortunate. My parents loved and encouraged me; my brother was empathetic and supportive; my friends (when I had them) were lots of fun."[68]

John did not find those friends until he was in high school, however. When he was a child his family settled in Orlando, Florida, and he was not very popular in school there. "I think I was quite difficult to be around," Green says. "My insecurity and anxiety made it difficult for me to have straightforward, engaging social interactions with anyone, and I was really super self-absorbed."[69] As a result, he spent most of his time alone. He was also bullied by the other boys, who would attack him both verbally and physically; for instance, he has painful memories of being thrown into a trash can. The experiences were both terrifying and dehumanizing, and the effects of these attacks would linger for weeks. "I'd just live in fear of that happening again," he remembers, "because I didn't feel like a person when it happened."[70]

On top of being socially awkward and bullied, John was not a good student; his grades were consistently in the low Cs. "I had always been told I was smart and had potential, but I had never shown the ability to deliver on it,"[71] he remembers. Part of the problem was that he saw no advantage to doing well in school. He remembers being eleven or twelve years old and thinking that the successful men he knew "literally put nooses [neckties] on themselves and then they went off to their jobs . . . That's not a recipe for a happy life."[72] At the time, John saw education as nothing more than jumping over a series of arbitrary hurdles that led only to a bleak future.

> "My insecurity and anxiety made it difficult for me to have straightforward, engaging social interactions with anyone, and I was really super self-absorbed."[69]
>
> —*John Green*

Finding His Tribe

Green's family had relatives who had attended Indian Springs School, a boarding school outside of Birmingham, Alabama. At fifteen, John asked to transfer there. He imagined he would have a better chance of making friends and doing well academically. His parents agreed, and John started at Indian Springs as a high school sophomore.

John had a wonderful experience at Indian Springs. Although he does not describe himself as popular, he found a community and made lots of friends. "I got to spend time with my peers in a relatively safe environment 24 hours a day, seven days a week, and that allowed me to have really intense, deep friendships,"[73] he says. He also developed a respect for learning that he had never had before. This, he realizes, was because he was suddenly part of a community of learners. "I found myself surrounded by people who celebrated intellectualism and engagement and who thought that my ironic, oh-so-cool disengagement wasn't clever or funny," he explains. "And so I started to learn, because learning was cool."[74]

Aspirations to the Priesthood

John loved to read and enjoyed writing. At Indian Springs his English teachers encouraged his writing and said he showed great promise. However, although he loved to write, he did not see becoming a writer as a realistic career path. He says, "I always thought being a writer was, like, being an astronaut or playing in the NFL or something. It always seemed to me a very unrealistic dream."[75]

Green also received encouragement for his writing at Kenyon College in Ohio, which he entered in 1995. But writing was not his sole focus in college; he was intensely interested in religion and wanted to become an Episcopal priest. He graduated from Kenyon with a dual major in English and religious studies and was accepted to the divinity school at the University of Chicago.

In preparation for becoming a priest, Green took a position as a chaplain at a children's hospital. Even though he was only twenty-two years old, most of his job entailed counseling parents whose children were dying or had just died. "I loved the work, and I doubt I'll ever do anything that important again," he explains. "But it really tore me apart. . . . I couldn't bear it. I didn't have the kind of faith that could encounter the truth of suffering without breaking."[76] One experience was particularly painful to him. A two-year-old girl had been rushed to the hospital with a severe skull fracture. She died, and the father—whom Green consoled and prayed with—later confessed that he was responsible for her injuries. "I didn't want him to be redeemed," Green wrote of the little girl's father. "I wanted, and want, [him] to suffer. If I could wish him peace, I could probably be a good chaplain."[77]

> "I always thought being a writer was, like, being an astronaut or playing in the NFL or something. It always seemed to me a very unrealistic dream."[75]
>
> —John Green

His True Calling

That experience was one among many that convinced Green that he was not suited for the priesthood. Instead, he continued to work on his writing and got a data entry job in Chicago at the American Library Association's book review magazine, *Booklist*. There, he caught the notice of a staff editor, Ilene Cooper. "He was a horrible slob, and he didn't do his job all that well," Cooper remembers. "But he was so engaging, and he would want to talk about things like our place in the universe."[78] Soon Green began reviewing books for the publication.

Cooper, who was also a young adult author, began helping him with what was to become his first novel, *Looking for Alaska* (2005). The novel is a coming-of-age story about first love, based on Green's experiences at Indian Springs. After a few rounds of edits, Cooper sent it to her publisher, and it was accepted. In 2006 it won the Michael L. Printz Award. His second novel, *An Abundance of Katherines* (2006), is also about teen romance and won the Printz Award in 2007. Green's career as a young adult novelist was taking off, and he decided it was time to devote himself to it full time. So when his wife, Sarah Urist-Green, was accepted to graduate school at Columbia University, he quit his job at *Booklist* and they moved to New York City.

Creating Community Online

Green was not happy in New York. He missed the community he had found at Indian Springs and later at *Booklist*. Without it, his writing career began to consume all of his energy and attention. Green felt like he was taking the business of writing and publishing too seriously. "I was right in the middle of my little pond," he says of the publishing world of New York. "It's good for some writers to be able to have constant conversations with peers about publishing, but I got this outsized sense of how important my pond was."[79]

Around this time, Green began noticing that communities were springing up on the Internet around online video

> "It's good for some writers to be able to have constant conversations with peers about publishing, but I got this outsized sense of how important my pond was."[79]
>
> —John Green

Nerdfighters Make an Unfinished Manuscript a Best Seller

In June 2011, when John Green announced online that he had a new book coming out, the community that had formed around his vlog, *Vlogbrothers*, was ecstatic. His fans, who called themselves Nerdfighters, immediately preordered the book en masse. Based on these preorders, the book immediately rose to number one on both the Amazon and Barnes & Noble best-seller lists—even though the publication date was six months away, the manuscript was not finished, and Green had not yet announced the title.

The book was *The Fault in Our Stars*, and Green promised that he would sign every single copy of the first printing. He wound up signing 150,000 copies of the book in a variety of marker colors chosen by the Nerdfighters. He said he decided to sign so many books because "1. I like my readers, and 2. I want to find a way to thank them for choosing to read my books in this media-saturated world, and 3. I can't tour everywhere, and it seems weird to preference readers who live near big metropolitan areas of the US over other readers, plus 4. I think it will be kind of fun unless my hand falls off." Green wound up needing physical therapy for his shoulder after completing the signing.

Quoted in Maryann Yin, "John Green to Sign 150,000 Copies of New Book," *GalleyCat* (blog), July 27, 2011. www .adweek.com.

blogs, or vlogs. He was especially impressed by *The Show* by Ze Frank, a daily vlog that encouraged its community of followers to make things together online. Green decided to launch a similar type of vlog with his brother, Hank. Since the brothers saw each other only once or twice a year, they decided to communicate via weekly YouTube videos. The topics of their videos cover a wide variety of subjects, from personal confessions to philosophical discussions to humorous rants. By 2007, the vlog, dubbed *Vlogbrothers*, had several thousand followers, and Green began to earn advertising money from the venture.

Green liked interacting with the eclectic community (who called themselves "Nerdfighters") that was forming around his vlog. The vlog and the projects it inspired—such as an online TV show about art and a documentary series for children—became Green's day job and his main source of income. By this time, the Greens had moved to Indianapolis so that Sarah, who had earned a master's degree in art history at Columbia, could take a job at the Indianapolis Museum of Art.

The Fault in Our Stars

While working on his online projects, Green continued to write and publish. In 2008 he published *Paper Towns*; in 2010 he published *Will Grayson, Will Grayson* with young adult author David Levithan. But one of his ideas had frustrated him for years. Green wanted to write about his time as a chaplain but felt he had no business as a healthy adult writing about the experiences of dying young people.

An encounter with one of the Nerdfighters, Esther Grace Earl, gave him a handle on the main character of what was to become *The Fault in Our Stars*. Esther, who was dying of thyroid cancer, struck up a conversation with Green at an event. She was funny, smart, brave, and angry about her illness. Green gave these traits to his main character, seventeen-year-old Hazel Grace Lancaster, who is dying of cancer. The story is about Hazel's tragic romance with Augustus Waters, a teenager from her support group whose cancer is in remission. Hazel and Augustus try to make sense of their lives and their illnesses while trying to come to terms with the fact that their love will soon be cut short. *The Fault in Our Stars* was published in 2012, two years after Esther's death at the age of sixteen. "I could not have written it without her friendship," Green says. "There is definitely something weird about her not being here to give her blessing or not."[80]

The Fault in Our Stars was a blockbuster hit and launched Green into young adult literature superstardom. In 2012, it debuted at number one on the *New York Times* best-seller list for children's chapter books and remained on the list for more than seventy-eight weeks. *Time* said of the book, "One doesn't like to throw around phrases like 'instant classic' lightly, but I can see *The Fault in Our Stars* taking its place alongside *Are You There God? It's Me, Margaret* [by Judy Blume] in the young-adult canon."[81] The book, which was made into a hit movie in 2014,

Fans clamor for Green's autograph in 2014—the year his popular book The Fault In Our Stars, became a hit movie. The book launched the author into young adult literature superstardom.

has over 30 million copies in print. Because of this success, in 2014 *Time* named Green one of the one hundred most influential people of the year.

Criticism for "Sick Lit"

Praise for *The Fault in Our Stars* was not universal, however. For instance, Tanith Carey of London's *Daily Mail* grouped the novel with other young adult books that deal with teenage illness, which she labeled "Sick Lit." She claimed that books like Green's "glamorize shocking life-and-death issues."[82] And because the book explores Hazel's belief that her illness makes her unattractive to boys, Carey also criticizes the novel for implying that what is most important to terminally ill young girls is whether or not boys will still like them.

Green took this criticism in stride, but he does not think that his novel glamorizes or trivializes suffering. "I don't agree with the idea that sick teenagers are less concerned with the big questions of the human head and the human heart than other teenagers,"[83]

Struggles with Mental Illness

John Green has been diagnosed with obsessive-compulsive disorder (OCD), a mental disorder characterized by obsessive thoughts, compulsive behaviors, anxiety, and depression. He says he has had "obsessive thought spirals for as long as I could remember," but his disorder is well managed with therapy and medication. During a relapse in 2015, he shared his thoughts and feelings online: "I have been reminded in the last several weeks just how painful and crushing this stuff can be," he tells his audience. "[But] there is hope. . . . How you feel when you are at your sickest is not how you will always feel."

Green has accepted his bouts of anxiety and obsessive thinking as a part of his personality. According to his wife, Sarah Urist-Green, Green's OCD is simply part of who he is and the way he experiences the world. Green even sees benefits to his condition. "From a novelist's perspective," he says, "the ability to cycle through all the possibilities and choose the worst is very helpful."

John Green, "On Mental Illness (and the End of Pizzamas)," YouTube, November 20, 2015. www.youtube.com /watch?v=Z_y4CACK-9g.

Quoted in Jodi Eichler-Levine, "The Blockbuster Spirituality of John Green's 'The Fault in Our Stars,'" *Religion Dispatches*, June 12, 2014. http://religiondispatches.org.

he explains. Young adult author Meg Rosoff agrees and claims that Green's genius is that he is able to accurately capture a teenager's emotional reality: feelings are big and dramatic, and love and tragedy often go hand in hand. "That's why his fans connect with him so perfectly and why he makes many adults uncomfortable," she says. "His specialty is longing rather than fulfillment."[84]

Looking for Alaska Banned from Schools

Though *Looking for Alaska* was published in 2005, it was not widely read until Green became a well-known young adult author. The story is about Miles "Pudge" Halter's experiences at a boarding school in Alabama, where Pudge is befriended by an eccentric group of students including the beautiful Alaska Young. Pudge has several romantic encounters with girls at the school, including Alaska, with whom he falls in love.

As the novel gained popularity, some adults became concerned about the explicit sexual content of the book. In 2015, the American Library Association reported that the novel was the most challenged book in the United States. (A book is "challenged" when parents demand that it be removed from libraries and school curriculums because of inappropriate content.) The passage that received the most objections concerned a bungled episode of oral sex between Pudge and his date, Lara. While the scene is explicit, Green notes that it is deliberately cold and clinical to contrast with a romantic kissing scene between Pudge and Alaska that follows it. "The novel is arguing . . . that emotionally intimate kissing can be a whole lot more fulfilling than emotionally empty oral sex,"[85] he explains. Green believes those who challenge the book are not giving teens enough credit. "Teenagers are critically engaged and thoughtful readers," he says. "They do not read *Looking for Alaska* and think 'I should go have some aggressively unerotic oral sex.'"[86] He is strongly against censorship and believes that decisions about what teens should read should be left to the experts—teachers and librarians.

> "That's why his fans connect with him so perfectly and why he makes many adults uncomfortable. . . . His specialty is longing rather than fulfillment."[84]
>
> —Young adult author Meg Rosoff.

Not Just a Novelist

Since publication of *The Fault in Our Stars*, Green has concentrated on his online projects, which have millions of followers. He assures his fans that his next novel is in the works, but he does not think of himself as primarily a novelist and considers his work online to be his day job. He uses his vlog and other online projects to educate teens and motivate them to create art and support charities. "I love reading and writing books," he says, "but it's difficult to use books to build communities that can tackle projects, which is something I really enjoy."[87] Even though his many activities sometimes pull him in different directions, they all have one thing in common—helping young people understand themselves and their world.

CHAPTER 6

Suzanne Collins

Suzanne Collins has made a career out of introducing young people to the philosophical and moral issues of war. She is the author of the wildly successful young adult trilogy *The Hunger Games*, which has sold more than 65 million copies in the United States alone and has spawned four blockbuster films. Collins's fantasy series for middle-school readers, *The Underland Chronicles*, also explores war-related themes, as does her picture book *Year of the Jungle*. Collins believes that it is important to discuss the realities of war with children. "You have young people at 18 who are enlisting in the army and they really don't have the slightest idea what they're getting into,"[88] she says. Through her fiction, Collins attempts to educate all ages of children about warfare and its consequences.

A Military Family

Suzanne Marie Collins was born on August 10, 1962, in Hartford, Connecticut. Her father, Lieutenant Colonel Michael John Collins, was a career US Air Force officer, and when Suzanne was six, he was deployed to Vietnam for a year. That event had a profound and long-lasting effect on young Suzanne. Even though her mother tried to shield her and her three older siblings from the realities of war that were broadcast on the news each night, she was still very afraid. "If your parent is deployed and you are that young, you spend the whole time wondering where they are and waiting for them to come home," she explains. "As time passes and the absence is longer and longer, you become more and more concerned—but you don't really have the words to express your concern."[89] The event changed Collins, and it marked the beginning of what was to become a lifelong interest in educating young people about warfare.

Her father was also changed by the war. For the rest of his life he had nightmares about his experiences in Vietnam, and Collins remembers being woken up by the sounds of him crying out during his dreams. Lt. Col. Collins, who was an expert on military history and had a PhD in political science, decided that rather than shield his children from the realities of war, he would teach them about it. "He, I think, felt it was his responsibility to make sure that all his children had an understanding about war, about its cost, its consequences,"[90] Collins explains. Her father spoke openly about his service and would frequently take the children to battlefields and war monuments—especially when they were stationed overseas in Belgium. Her father "would start back with whatever had precipitated the war and moved up through the battlefield you were standing in,"[91] Collins remembers. Her dad was a good teacher, and Suzanne found these discussions very interesting.

> "If your parent is deployed and you are that young, you spend the whole time wondering where they are and waiting for them to come home."[89]
>
> —Suzanne Collins

A Gifted Screenwriter

Because her father was a career military officer, Collins's family moved around a lot when she was young. In addition to their time overseas in Belgium, they lived in Indiana; New York City; and West Point, New York, where her father taught military history at

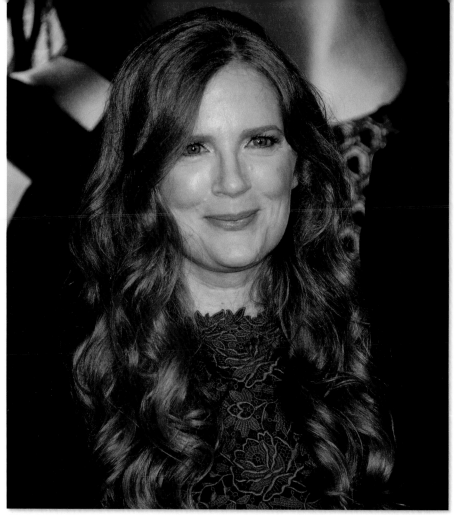

Suzanne Collins (pictured in 2013) wrote the wildly successful young adult trilogy The Hunger Games. *Through her fiction, Collins introduces young people to the philosophical and moral issues of war.*

the US Military Academy. Some of Suzanne's earliest memories were of the young men in uniform drilling at West Point. The family eventually moved to Alabama, and in 1980 Suzanne graduated from high school at the Alabama School of Fine Arts. She went to college at Indiana University, where she met her future husband, Cap Pryor, an actor. She graduated in 1985 with a double major in theater and telecommunications and set her sights on being a screenwriter. She and Pryor, with whom she later had two children, moved to New York when Collins was twenty-five so that she could pursue a master of fine arts in dramatic writing at New York University.

In 1991, Collins got her first job as a screenwriter, writing for children's television shows. She quickly moved up through the ranks and worked on many successful shows, including the Emmy-nominated *Clarissa Explains It All* and *The Mystery Files of Shelby Woo*. She also wrote for the preschool set, creating episodes for *Little Bear* and *Oswald* and cowriting the Christmas special *Santa, Baby!* which was nominated for a Writers Guild of America Award.

Collins's work in television was noticed by James Proimos, the creator of the children's program *Generation O!* He hired her as head writer and the two became friends. Proimos, who also wrote and illustrated children's books, was impressed by Collins's writing, and he suggested that she try her hand at novels. "She seemed like a book writer to me; it was sort of her personality," said Proimos. "She also had the style and the mind of a novelist."[92] He urged her to think of the future—television is historically a young person's business, but novelists are not penalized as they age. Collins, who was then in her thirties, took what he said to heart and began to plan what was to become a five-part series for middle-school readers, *The Underland Chronicles.*

The Underland Chronicles

The first novel in *The Underland Chronicles* series, *Gregor the Overlander*, is about an eleven-year-old boy who falls through a sewer grate in New York City and discovers an underworld where humans coexist with giant humanlike cockroaches, rats, and other sewer-dwelling creatures. Collins's inspiration for the book was *Alice's Adventures in Wonderland*; she was living in New York City and thinking about how unfamiliar the pastoral setting of Lewis Carroll's classic novel must seem to city kids. What if, she thought, Alice were to fall down a manhole instead of a rabbit hole?

She discussed the concept with Proimos, who was so taken with the idea that he referred her to his literary agent, Rosemary Stimola. Stimola asked for a sample chapter and was impressed with the result. "Quite honestly, I knew from the very first paragraph I had a very gifted writer," said Stimola. "She established a character I cared about. She established a story and a mood that touched my heart."[93] Stimola offered to represent Collins before she had even finished a first draft, which is unusual in publishing. Collins accepted.

In *Gregor the Overlander*, Collins began to explore her interest in the moral implications of war. She called her father for help, and the two conceived an underground war in the sewers of New York, with realistic military strategies and alliances. "We had two superpowers, the humans and the bats," Collins said, "but the humans were dependent on the alliance with the bats, because then they became aerial fighters."[94] At the core of the novel was a variation on a common topic of war narratives: the rescue of a prisoner of war.

Gregor the Overlander was published in 2003 to rave reviews and won multiple awards. It was a *USA Today* best seller, was named the *Kirkus Reviews* Editor's Choice in 2003, and won the 2004 New Atlantic Independent Book Sellers' Children's Novel Award. Of the novel, *Horn Book* magazine wrote, "The fast-paced, detailed narrative features vivid battle scenes . . . dangerous alliances, some frightening close calls, and the sobering death of comrades-in-arms."[95] *Booklist* gave it a starred review, calling it an "exceptional debut novel."[96] Unfortunately Collins's father passed away before the book was published.

> "I knew from the very first paragraph I had a very gifted writer. . . . She established a character I cared about. She established a story and a mood that touched my heart."[93]
>
> —Literary agent Rosemary Stimola.

Necessary Versus Unnecessary War

Collins went on to write four more books in *The Underland Chronicles* series, which were published between 2004 and 2007. These novels explore other facets of warfare, including assassination, biological weapons, genocide, and the role of military intelligence. Collins does not think that these themes are too adult for children. "There are children soldiers all around the world right now who are 9, 10, carrying arms, forced to be at war," she says. "Can our children not even read a fictional story about it? I think they can."[97]

Adults Love *The Hunger Games*, Too

Part of the success of *The Hunger Games* is due to its appeal to both young adults and adults—a trend that began in earnest with J.K. Rowling's *Harry Potter* books. Damien Walter, a columnist for Britain's *Guardian*, believes that Collins's books appeal to adults in part because evil is equated with the adult world, which Walter calls "dysfunctional." He writes that the world of *The Hunger Games* is "an adult world of political and economic repression," and that the fight against it corresponds with adults' urge to fight back against "a vast burden of debt [and] a crushing, meaningless job in a corporate bureaucracy." Others have credited the series' appeal to the fact that it makes adults feel better about their own reality. As *New York Daily News* blogger Lauren Sarner explains, "As our own reality becomes darker, we turn to fiction for escape. . . . [These] novels allow us [adults] to say, 'well, our reality may be bad, but at least it's not that bad!'"

Damien Walter, "Young Adult Fiction Is Loved Because It Speaks to Us All—Unlike Adult Stories," *Guardian* (Manchester, UK), September 19, 2014. www.theguardian.com.

Lauren Sarner, "Dystopian Fiction, and Its Appeal: Why Do Apocalyptic Portrayals of Existence Dominate Teen Shelves?," *New York Daily News*, June 28, 2013. www.nydailynews.com.

The series also addresses the idea of unnecessary versus necessary war—a theme that is at the heart of much of Collins's fiction. She believes that the question of whether war was necessary or unnecessary was something that her father spent his life thinking about—both as a soldier and as an expert in military history. It was also a question that he encouraged his children to examine on a regular basis. "If I took the 40 years of my dad talking to me about war and battles and taking me to battlefields and distilled it down into one question, it would probably be the idea of the necessary or unnecessary war,"[98] Collins explains. She says that the central conflict in *The Underland Chronicles* shows how unnecessary wars can unfortunately become necessary wars if they are not stopped in time. "[It] is an unnecessary war for a very long time until it becomes a necessary war," she says of the conflict in the series, "because there have been all these points where people could have gotten off the train but they didn't. They just kept moving the violence forward until it's gone out of control."[99]

Origins of *The Hunger Games*

The idea of necessary versus unnecessary war also became the central theme of her next series: *The Hunger Games*. Collins conceived of the story while watching television late one night. She was flipping through the channels, switching between a real-ity television show and coverage of the war in Iraq. In the reality program, young people were competing with each other; in the news story, young people were fighting in an actual war. "I was really tired," she remembers, "and the lines between these stories started to blur in a very unsettling way. That's the moment when Katniss's [the series' heroine] story came to me."[100]

The Hunger Games features a televised competition among young people orchestrated by a conquering government. It is a gladiator story, and the games are fought to the death. Collins

High school students in Southern California follow along during an in-class reading of Catching Fire, *the second book in* The Hunger Games *trilogy. Although the books contain graphic violence, teachers say nonviolence is actually the series' theme.*

admits that this aspect of the story was inspired by the 1960 film *Spartacus*, which she had loved as a child. In the film, a slave escapes gladiator school and becomes the leader of a slave rebellion. Collins's father had put the story into context by reading young Suzanne the historical account of Spartacus from Plutarch's *Parallel Lives*, and it made a big impression on her. "I think I was destined at some point to write a gladiator game,"[101] she explains.

Greek mythology also inspired the *The Hunger Games* trilogy—in particular, the myth of Theseus and the Minotaur, which Collins read when she was eight. In the myth, after Crete conquers Athens, every nine years the king of Crete forces Athens to deliver fourteen boys and girls to be devoured by the Minotaur, a monster with the body of a man and the head of a bull. "Even when I was a little kid, the story took my breath away, because it was so cruel, and Crete was so ruthless," Collins remembers. "The message is, mess with us and we'll do something worse than kill you—we'll kill your children."[102] Collins combined both ideas—the sacrifice of children by a conquered people and a gladiator's rebellion against slavery—in *The Hunger Games* trilogy, which tracks Katniss's journey from a participant in the games to the leader of a rebellion against a totalitarian government. Like that in *The Underland Chronicles*, the conflict in *The Hunger Games* trilogy progresses from an unnecessary war (a gladiator competition among children) to a necessary one (the rebellion against slavery).

> "I think I was destined at some point to write a gladiator game."[101]
>
> —*Suzanne Collins*

Too Violent for Younger Readers?

The first novel in the trilogy, *The Hunger Games*, was published in 2008 and became a *New York Times* best seller. The second, *Catching Fire*, was published in 2009, and the third, *Mockingjay*, came out in 2010. All three award-winning novels were on multiple adult and young adult best-seller lists. Though the books were recommended for children thirteen and up, they became very popular with younger readers. They were also embraced by teachers for their antiwar message, and some teachers even assigned the book to students younger than thirteen.

Because the novels contain a great deal of violence, some parents were concerned about the effect that violence would have on younger readers. Carol Lloyd, executive editor of the website GreatSchools, was especially concerned about her daughter's reaction to the book—which had been recommended to her by her sixth-grade teacher. As her daughter became obsessed with quoting and acting out parts of the novel, Lloyd writes, "I couldn't help wondering what the hyperbolic violence was doing to her brain."[103] While Lloyd does not condemn *The Hunger Games* outright, she says that educators who embrace graphic violence in young adult fiction seem to be "hell-bent on using violent extremes to engender a love of reading."[104] Other critics of the novel tried to get it removed from school reading lists, claiming the violence was too graphic and intense for even teenaged readers.

Most educators see the violence in *The Hunger Games* as appropriate for its subject matter and believe it serves to emphasize a nonviolent message. Collins insists that she is primarily writing about war, and when writing about war, it is necessary to realistically portray its costs, which are both violent and emotionally disturbing. If an author is not willing to do that, Collins believes, he or she should "go write another kind of story."[105]

A Picture Book About War

In 2013 Collins completed what she says is "a larger goal I have, which is to write a war-appropriate story for every age of kids."[106] Her picture book, *Year of the Jungle*, is an autobiographical account of the year when her father was stationed in Vietnam. As six-year-old Suzanne wonders and worries about what is happening to her father in the jungle, she gradually comes to understand what it means when a parent is deployed in a war. Collins had the idea in the back of her mind for years but did not know how to execute it. "My fear was, with the subject matter, the impulse would be to make the art dark and very serious,"[107] she explains. However, her friend James Proimos offered to illustrate the book,

A Resurgence of Dystopian Fiction

The Hunger Games belongs to a genre known as dystopian fiction: stories set in a bleak future that embodies ideas that contrast with the story's core values. (In the case of *The Hunger Games*, those values are economic, political, and personal freedom for all.) While many young adult novels portray a dystopian future, some experts have said the success of *The Hunger Games* is responsible for reinvigorating the genre. For instance, both James Dashner's *The Maze Runner* (2009) and Veronica Roth's *Divergent* (2011) became best-selling young adult series—in print and on the big screen—and countless other young adult authors have seen success with dystopian scenarios. However, Collins believes that the success of *The Hunger Games* did not create interest in dystopian fiction; instead, it simply happened to be the first to harness general concerns in the culture. "I just think the dystopian stories are striking a nerve with people right now," she says. "I think people respond to dystopian stories because they're ways of acting out anxieties that we have and fears that we have about the future."

Quoted in Lev Grossman, "'Come for the Love Story, Stay for the War': A Conversation with Suzanne Collins and Francis Lawrence," *Time*, November 22, 2013. http://entertainment.time.com.

and Collins was pleased with his ideas. She hopes the book will help young children cope when a parent is deployed overseas.

A Private Person

Since 2009, Collins has been involved in working on the successful *Hunger Games* franchise of films. She has stated that there will be no more *Hunger Games* books, and she has not announced that she has any new projects in the works. A private person who rarely grants interviews, Collins currently lives in Connecticut with her husband.

After the final *Hunger Games* film was released in 2015, Collins wrote a letter thanking everyone who had been involved in the films over the years. She writes that she is pleased that the films have stayed true to the themes she introduced in the novels and that they have helped her "introduce the ideas of just war theory to young audiences."[108] Collins hopes that her body of work will help children and teens of all ages better understand the realities of war.

SOURCE NOTES

Introduction: The New Golden Age of Young Adult Literature

1. Quoted in Shelley Diaz, "YA: A Category for the Masses. But What About Teens?," *School Library Journal*, November 3, 2015. www.slj.com.
2. Quoted in Shelley Diaz, "Embracing Diversity in YA Lit," *School Library Journal*, September 12, 2013. www.slj.com.
3. Quoted in Diaz, "YA."

Chapter 1: Walter Dean Myers

4. Quoted in Shannon Maughan, "Obituary: Walter Dean Myers," *Publishers Weekly*, July 2, 2014. www.publishersweekly.com.
5. Walter Dean Myers, *Bad Boy: A Memoir*. New York: HarperCollins, 2001, p. 46.
6. Quoted in Jennifer Brown, "Walter Dean Myers Unites Two Passions," *Publishers Weekly*, March 22, 1999. www.publishersweekly.com.
7. Walter Dean Myers, "Where Are the People of Color in Children's Books?," *New York Times*, March 15, 2014. www.nytimes.com.
8. Myers, *Bad Boy*, p. 196.
9. Myers, *Bad Boy*, p. 200.
10. Myers, *Bad Boy*, p. 202.
11. Myers, "Where Are the People of Color in Children's Books?"
12. Walter Dean Myers, "Walter Dean Myers," *Interviewly*, December 2013. http://interviewly.com.

13. Myers, "Where Are the People of Color in Children's Books?"
14. Quoted in Dashka Slater, "Walter Dean Myers," Walter Dean Myers. http://walterdeanmyers.net.

Chapter 2: J.K. Rowling
15. J.K. Rowling, "The Not Especially Fascinating Life So Far of J.K. Rowling," Accio Quote!, February 16, 2007. www.accio-quote.org.
16. Quoted in "J.K. Rowling, Harry Potter Creator, Says She Was Bullied as a Teen," *Huffington Post*, September 17, 2011. www.huffingtonpost.com.
17. Quoted in "J.K. Rowling's Biography from A&E, Part 1 of 4," YouTube, December 22, 2010. www.youtube.com/watch?v=ycrLE46w6tY.
18. Quoted in Meredith Vieira, "Harry Potter: The Final Chapter," *Dateline* [transcript], July 30, 2007. www.nbcnews.com.
19. Quoted in Ian Parker, "Mugglemarch," *New Yorker*, October 2012. www.newyorker.com.
20. Quoted in John Lawless, "Revealed: The Eight-Year-Old Girl Who Saved Harry Potter," *New Zealand Herald*, July 3, 2005. www.nzherald.co.nz.
21. Quoted in Parker, "Mugglemarch."
22. Quoted in Devaksha Vallabhjee, "Oprah Talks to J.K. Rowling," *Oprah Magazine*, May 2014. www.oprahmag.co.za.
23. Quoted in ChristianAnswers.net, "Is the 'Harry Potter . . .' Series Truly Harmless?," February 1, 2002. www.christiananswers.net.
24. Judy Blume, "Is Harry Potter Evil?," *New York Times*, October 22, 1999. www.nytimes.com.
25. Quoted in David Smith, "Potter's Magic Spell Turns Boys into Bookworms," *Observer* (London), July 9, 2005. www.theguardian.com.
26. Quoted in Vallabhjee, "Oprah Talks to J.K. Rowling."

Chapter 3: Nnedi Okorafor
27. Quoted in Fleur Clarke, "Read an Extract from Nnedi Okorafor's *Binti*," Hodderscape, September 24, 2015. www.hodderscape.co.uk.
28. Quoted in Bryan Thomas Schmidt, "SFFWRTCHT: A Chat with Author Nnedi Okorafor," *Grasping for the Wind*, August 4, 2011. www.graspingforthewind.com.
29. Quoted in Jeremy L.C. Jones, "If It Scares You, Write It: A Conversation with Nnedi Okorafor," *Clarkesworld*. http://clarkesworldmagazine.com.
30. Nnedi Okorafor, interviewed by David Barr Kirtley, "Nnedi Okorafor Interview—Geek's Guide to the Galaxy Podcast #21," YouTube, September 29, 2012. www.youtube.com/watch?v=Q56zccBd0_k.

31. Quoted in Mikki Kendall, "A Nigerian Sorceress Makes Her Way," *Publishers Weekly*, April 12, 2010. www.publishersweekly.com.
32. Quoted in Hannah Onifade, "Exclusive Interview with Nigerian Science Fiction Writer, Nnedi Okoroafor [*sic*]," Ventures Africa, September 23, 2015. http://venturesafrica.com.
33. Nnedi Okorafor, interviewed by Sarah Culberson, "Nnedi Okorafor on the Africa Channel's 'Behind the Words' Part 1," YouTube, December 29, 2010. www.youtube.com/watch?v=Vboc3UVVTk8.
34. Quoted in "Nnedi Okorafor, Shared Worlds' 2011 Amazon Guest Author," Shared Worlds, 2011. www.wofford.edu.
35. Quoted in Charles Tan, "Nnedi Okorafor Interview on the Nebula Awards Website," *Nnedi's Wahala Zone* (blog), December 9, 2008. http://nnedi.blogspot.com.
36. Okorafor, "Nnedi Okorafor Interview—Geek's Guide to the Galaxy Podcast #21."
37. Quoted in *Locus Online*, "Nnedi Okorafor: Between Cultures," December 2007. www.locusmag.com.
38. Quoted in Varian Johnson, "Nnedi Okorafor-Mbachu," *Brown Bookshelf*, February 13, 2008. http://thebrownbookshelf.com.
39. Nnedi Okorafor, "Zahrah the Windseeker Wins the Black Excellence Award for Outstanding Achievement in Literature (Fiction)," *Nnedi's Wahala Zone* (blog), October 30, 2012. http://nnedi.blogspot.com.
40. Quoted in "Zahrah the Windseeker." http://nnedi.com.
41. Okorafor, "Nnedi Okorafor Interview—Geek's Guide to the Galaxy Podcast #21."
42. Quoted in *Locus Online*, "Nnedi Okorafor: Magical Futurism," May 2015. www.locusmag.com.
43. Quoted in *Locus Online*, "Nnedi Okorafor: Magical Futurism."

Chapter 4: Rainbow Rowell

44. Quoted in Neda Ulaby, "Rainbow Rowell Does Romance with a Subversive (Read: Realistic) Twist," NPR, July 7, 2014. www.npr.org.
45. "Leigh Bardugo Interviews Rainbow Rowell at BookCon 2015," YouTube, June 5, 2015. www.youtube.com/watch?v=yM3ky_EgnZY.
46. Quoted in Ashley Ford, "How Rainbow Rowell Turned a Bomb into a Best-Selling Novel," BuzzFeed, August 7, 2014. www.buzzfeed.com.
47. Quoted in Ford, "How Rainbow Rowell Turned a Bomb into a Best-Selling Novel."
48. Quoted in Casey Gilly, "Rainbow Rowell Talks to CBLDF About the Attack on *Eleanor & Park*," Comic Book Legal Defense Fund, September 27, 2013. http://cbldf.org.

49. Quoted in Ford, "How Rainbow Rowell Turned a Bomb into a Best-Selling Novel."

50. Quoted in Figment, "Breaking the Mold: Rainbow Rowell on YA and Body Image," March 5, 2013. http://dailyfig.figment.com.

51. Quoted in Ford, "How Rainbow Rowell Turned a Bomb into a Best-Selling Novel."

52. Quoted in Nathan Maharaj, "Kobo in Conversation: Rainbow Rowell," YouTube, November 25, 2013. www.youtube.com/watch?v=ujDz PSib8wI.

53. Shreeja Ravindranathan, "Rainbow Rowell: I'm a Better Reader than a Writer," *Friday Magazine*, June 24, 2014.

54. Detroit Public TV, "Rainbow Rowell Discusses *Carry On* at Book Expo America," YouTube, June 5, 2015. www.youtube.com/watch?v=qXam-1r_QcQ.

55. John Green, "Two Against the World," *New York Times*, March 8, 2013. www.nytimes.com.

56. Quoted in Figment, "Breaking the Mold."

57. Quoted in Gilly, "Rainbow Rowell Talks to CBLDF About the Attack on *Eleanor & Park*."

58. Quoted in Gilly, "Rainbow Rowell Talks to CBLDF About the Attack on *Eleanor & Park*."

59. Quoted in Gilly, "Rainbow Rowell Talks to CBLDF About the Attack on *Eleanor & Park*."

60. Linda Holmes, "True Love, Book Fights, and Why Ugly Stories Matter," *Monkey See* (blog), September 19, 2013. www.npr.org.

61. Julie Blaha, "Statement to the A-H School Board on *Eleanor & Park* Book Selection," AHEM Weekly Updates, September 23, 2013. http://ahemweekly.blogspot.com.

62. Quoted in Shannon Prather, "After Book Challenge at Anoka High, District Revises Policies," *Star Tribune* (Minneapolis), March 27, 2014. www.startribune.com.

63. Quoted in Goodreads, "Interview with Rainbow Rowell," December 2013. www.goodreads.com.

64. Quoted in Maharaj, "Kobo in Conversation."

65. Quoted in Detroit Public TV, "Leigh Bardugo Interviews Rainbow Rowell at BookCon 2015," YouTube, June 5, 2015. www.youtube.com/watch?v=yM3ky_EgnZY.

66. Quoted in Amanda Green, "*The Rumpus* Interview with Rainbow Rowell," *Rumpus*, October 17, 2014. http://therumpus.net.

67. Quoted in Detroit Public TV, "Rainbow Rowell Discusses *Carry On* at Book Expo America."

Chapter 5: John Green

68. Quoted in Deborah Takahashi, "*The Fault in Our Stars* by John Green (Read by Kate Rudd)," *Kazumi Reads*, August 21, 2013. http://ladykazumi.blogspot.com.

69. John Green, "Biographical Questions." http://johngreenbooks.com.

70. John Green, "John Green—Being Bullied," Bystander Revolution, 2015. www.bystanderrevolution.org.

71. Quoted in Margaret Talbot, "The Teen Whisperer," *New Yorker*, June 9, 2014. www.newyorker.com.

72. John Green, "The Nerd's Guide to Learning Everything Online," TEDxIndianapolis, November 2012. www.ted.com.

73. Quoted in Bob Carlton, "Before 'The Fault in Our Stars,' John Green Was an 'Awkward' Student in Indian Springs, Alabama," Al.com, June 6, 2014. www.al.com.

74. Green, "The Nerd's Guide to Learning Everything Online."

75. Green, "Biographical Questions."

76. Quoted in Eisha Prather and Jules Danielson, "Seven Impossible Interviews Before Breakfast #19: John Green—Printz Winner, Nerd Fighter, WorldSuck Decreaser," *Seven Impossible Things Before Breakfast* (blog), Blaine.org, April 13, 2007. http://blaine.org.

77. John Green, "Nick (from All Things Considered)," May 26, 2003. http://johngreenbooks.com.

78. Quoted in Talbot, "The Teen Whisperer."

79. Quoted in Emma Brokes, "John Green: Teenager, Aged 36," *Intelligent Life Magazine*, May/June 2014. www.intelligentlifemagazine.com.

80. Quoted in Talbot, "The Teen Whisperer."

81. Lev Grossman, "The Topic of Cancer," *Time*, February 6, 2012. http://content.time.com.

82. Tanith Carey, "The 'Sick-Lit' Books Aimed at Children: It's a Disturbing Phenomenon. Tales of Teenage Cancer, Self-Harm and Suicide. . .," *Daily Mail* (London), January 2, 2013. www.dailymail.co.uk.

83. Quoted in Brokes, "John Green."

84. Quoted in Brokes, "John Green."

85. John Green, "On the Banning of *Looking for Alaska*," *Vlogbrothers* (video blog), April 12, 2016. www.youtube.com/watch?v=69rd -7vEF3s.

86. Green, "On the Banning of *Looking for Alaska*."

87. Quoted in Stacey Hayman, "Wouldn't You Like to Know . . . John Green," *Voya Magazine*, October 19, 2012. www.voyamagazine .com.

Chapter 6: Suzanne Collins

88. Quoted in Lev Grossman, "'I Was Destined to Write a Gladiator Game': A Conversation with Suzanne Collins and Francis Lawrence," *Time*, November 20, 2013. http://entertainment.time.com.

89. Quoted in Susan Dominus, "Suzanne Collins's War Stories for Kids," *New York Times Magazine*, April 8, 2011. www.nytimes.com.

90. Quoted in Lev Grossman, "Writing 'War-Appropriate' Stories for Kids: A Conversation with Suzanne Collins and Francis Lawrence," *Time*, November 19, 2013. http://entertainment.time.com.

91. Quoted in Hillel Italie, "How Has 'Hunger Games' Author Suzanne Collins' Life Changed?," *Huffington Post*, May 25, 2011. www.huff ingtonpost.com.

92. Quoted in Italie, "How Has 'Hunger Games' Author Suzanne Collins' Life Changed?"

93. Quoted in Tom Henthorne, *Approaching "The Hunger Games" Trilogy: A Literary and Cultural Analysis*. Jefferson, NC: McFarland, 2012, p. 16.

94. Quoted in Dominus, "Suzanne Collins's War Stories for Kids."

95. Quoted in "Gregor the Overlander." www.suzannecollinsbooks .com.

96. Quoted in "Gregor the Overlander."

97. Quoted in Grossman, "'I Was Destined to Write a Gladiator Game.'"

98. Quoted in Grossman, "Writing 'War-Appropriate' Stories for Kids."

99. Quoted in Grossman, "Writing 'War-Appropriate' Stories for Kids."

100. Quoted in Rick Margolis, "A Killer Story: An Interview with Suzanne Collins, Author of 'The Hunger Games,'" *School Library Journal*, September 1, 2008. www.slj.com.

101. Quoted in Grossman, "'I Was Destined to Write a Gladiator Game.'"

102. Quoted in Margolis, "A Killer Story."

103. Carol Lloyd, "Help! My Child Has Been Reaped," GreatKids! www .greatschools.org.

104. Lloyd, "Help! My Child Has Been Reaped."

105. Quoted in "Suzanne Collins on Writing *The Hunger Games* and More," *Inner Writer* (blog). http://theinnerwriter.com.

106. Quoted in Grossman, "Writing 'War-Appropriate' Stories for Kids."

107. Suzanne Collins, "A Conversation with Suzanne Collins and James Proimos," video, Scholastic. www.scholastic.com.

108. Suzanne Collins, "Letter from Suzanne Collins: A Thank You to *The Hunger Games* Film Team," *On Our Minds* (blog), November 17, 2015. http://oomscholasticblog.com.

FOR FURTHER RESEARCH

Books

Kathleen Deakin, Laura Brown, and James Blasingame Jr., *John Green: Teen Whisperer*. Lanham, MD: Rowman & Littlefield, 2015.

Tom Henthorne, *Approaching "The Hunger Games" Trilogy: A Literary and Cultural Analysis*. Jefferson, NC: McFarland, 2012.

Nnedi Okorafor, *Akata Witch 2: Breaking Kola*. New York: Penguin, 2016.

Rainbow Rowell, *Carry On*. New York: St. Martin's, 2015.

Mark Shapiro, *J.K. Rowling: The Wizard Behind Harry Potter*. New York: St. Martin's, 2007.

Mary Ellen Snodgrass, *Walter Dean Myers: A Literary Companion*. Jefferson, NC: McFarland, 2006.

Internet Sources

Lev Grossman, "Katniss Is 'A Wreck': A Conversation with Suzanne Collins and Francis Lawrence," *Time*, November 18, 2013. http://entertainment.time.com/2013/11/18/catching-up-with-catching-fire-a-conversation-with-suzanne-collins-and-francis-lawrence.

Lev Grossman, "Writing 'War-Appropriate' Stories for Kids: A Conversation with Suzanne Collins and Francis Lawrence," *Time*, November 19, 2013. http://entertainment.time.com/2013/11/19/writing-war

-appropriate-stories-for-kids-a-conversation-with-suzanne-collins
-and-francis-lawrence.

Lev Grossman, "'I Was Destined to Write a Gladiator Game': A Conversation with Suzanne Collins and Francis Lawrence," *Time*, November 20, 2013. http://entertainment.time.com/2013/11/20/i-was-destined-to-write-a-gladiator-game-a-conversation-with-suzanne-collins-and-francis-lawrence.

Lev Grossman, "'I'm More Like Plutarch than Katniss': A Conversation with Suzanne Collins and Francis Lawrence," November 21, 2013. http://entertainment.time.com/2013/11/21/im-more-like-plutarch-than-katniss-a-conversation-with-suzanne-collins-and-francis-lawrence.

Lev Grossman, "Come for the Love Story, Stay for the War: A Conversation with Suzanne Collins and Francis Lawrence," November 22, 2013. http://entertainment.time.com/2013/11/22/come-for-the-love-story-stay-for-the-war-a-conversation-with-suzanne-collins-and-francis-lawrence.

Websites

J.K. Rowling (www.jkrowling.com). The official website of J.K. Rowling, this site contains biographical information, essays, trivia, and descriptions of all of J.K. Rowling's works.

John Green (www.johngreenbooks.com). John Green's website contains biographical information, news, descriptions of Green's fiction and essays, and links to all of his online projects, including videos, vlogs, and others.

Nnedi Okorafor (www.nnedi.com). Nnedi Okorafor's website contains information about the author and her works, links to stories and essays published online, and a link to her blog, *Nnedi's Wahala Zone*.

Rainbow Rowell (www.rainbowrowell.com). Rainbow Rowell's website includes biographical information, descriptions of Rowell's works, FAQs, news, and links to interviews.

Suzanne Collins (www.suzannecollinsbooks.com). Suzanne Collins's website contains biographical information, interviews, and information about her works.

Walter Dean Myers (www.walterdeanmyers.net). The official website of Walter Dean Myers, the site contains information about the author and his works, links to videos and interviews, and information for parents and teachers.

INDEX

PICTURE CREDITS

ABOUT THE AUTHOR

Christine Wilcox writes fiction and nonfiction for young adults and adults. She has worked as an editor, an instructional designer, and a writing instructor. She lives in Richmond, Virginia, with her husband, David, and her son, Doug.